*Computers and Information Systems
in Education*

JOHN I. GOODLAD
University of California, Los Angeles
AND
Institute for Development of Educational Activities

JOHN F. O'TOOLE, JR.
System Development Corporation, Santa Monica

LOUISE L. TYLER
University of California, Los Angeles

Computers
and
Information Systems
in
Education

Harcourt, Brace & World, Inc.

New York / Chicago / Burlingame

Preface

For the initiated, especially those who have in some way linked their careers to computers, visions of the potential services of electronic data processing (EDP) in education are highly exhilarating. But for the uninitiated, visions of a computer's potential are somewhat unsettling, partly because they are blurred by lack of familiarity with how computers work. The purpose of *Computers and Information Systems in Education* is to sharpen the focus a little for the uninitiated educator and the interested layman by describing the present and potential applications of EDP in education. The book is also intended to help specialists in EDP to understand current educational problems so they can better assist educators in setting up information systems. The book is not intended for the specialist in EDP who is also knowledgeable in education, nor is this a casebook of practices and methods.

Instead, this volume describes how computers and electronic accounting machines work and what they can and cannot do. The book discusses the routine uses of EDP for business and student accounting, as well as the innovative uses of EDP in education—for simulation techniques, computerized scheduling, computer-based teaching machines, rapid document-retrieval systems, etc. This volume also discusses the traditional responsibilities the educator must continue to assume even in the computer age, as well as the new roles that are created for the educator by the computer. To illustrate our discussions, we describe many of the educational information systems now in operation across the country. In addition, Appendix B describes twenty-seven state, regional, and local educational data processing systems, indicating their current and prospective applications, the names of key personnel, and pertinent financial data.

We began the groundwork for this book by sponsoring, in collaboration with others, a conference of specialists in educational data processing, teachers, curriculum and guidance specialists, school administrators, psychologists, and research workers. Appendix A provides the names and professional affiliations of the twenty-seven participants in this conference, held at the Lake Arrowhead Conference Center of the University of California. Our work continued, again with collaborators, with the analysis of the literature in the field, visits to computer-based information processing centers, and the perusal of many reports from users of EDP in education. This work, supported by the Cooperative Research Program of the Office of Education, United States Department of Health, Education and Welfare (Project No. F–026), was summarized in *Application of Electronic Data Processing Methods in Education,* a report forwarded to the Office of Education in 1965.

Substantial portions of that report, especially of the first two chapters and the Appendices, are included here. However, much of the material has been updated and reorganized, some chapters have been combined and rewritten, and new material has been included throughout. Only we three, therefore, can be held responsible for the present volume.

We are grateful to the United States Office of Education for the allocation of funds to prepare our 1965 report. We also appreciate the time and resources made available by U.C.L.A., the System Development Corporation, and the Kettering Foundation to sustain our most recent activities. We extend our thanks to Donald D. Bushnell of the Brooks Foundation, John G. Caffrey of the System Development Corporation, and Arthur N. Thayer of the Timber School District, Newbury Park, California, who were prime movers in bringing about the Lake Arrowhead Conference; Mr. Caffrey was also a co-author of the 1965 report, and Mr. Bushnell wrote sections of it.

We also thank Fred L. Converse of the System Development Corporation for the preparation of Appendix B of this book and Mr. Caffrey for his contributions to Chapters 2 and 3. Finally, we are grateful to Elizabeth McKinstry and Arline Duff for typing the final manuscript.

JOHN I. GOODLAD / JOHN F. O'TOOLE, JR. / LOUISE L. TYLER

Contents

Computers and Information Systems
in Education

The great, metallic beast . . .
The genie we have raised to rule the earth,
Obsequious to our will
But servant-master still,
The tireless serf already half a god . . .

—STEPHEN VINCENT BENET

1

Education and Computer Technology: An Overview

A precocious infant scarcely out of swaddling clothes has moved relentlessly and inescapably into our lives. The electronic computer, mainstay of an advancing information technology, is significantly altering a wide range of human affairs. Limited mainly by the resourcefulness of its user, the computer is viewed by some as a potentially dynamic force for meeting the rapidly changing needs of society, for eradicating social ills such as poverty, and for freeing all men to engage in pursuits once thought to be the exclusive domain of an elite few. It is viewed by others as a threat to the very existence of mankind.

What is this pseudohuman, possessing apparently vast potentialities for good or evil, just as man himself possesses these dual propensities? Our first lesson on the computer—one we must never forget—is that the machine derives its potentialities from man himself.

Picture a room full of specialized clerical workers. The work to be done in the "Room" is inserted through a window marked IN and the results emerge from a window marked OUT. The

3

workers in the Room are superbly skilled at their highly specialized work, but they are obliged to do neither more nor less than what they are told. Any work to be done must be accompanied by detailed instructions, written in a precise language whose small vocabulary consists of terms such as add, subtract, multiply, divide, and compare. The workers in the Room make no decisions themselves but operate according to fixed rules. For example, they may compare two words or numbers and determine whether they are identical. The instructions for the problem must specify clearly what is then to be done if the values are equal or unequal. The way in which the results of the work done in the Room are to be arranged upon emerging from the OUT window must also be specified in advance. If a set of instructions contains erroneous or contradictory rules, or if an unanticipated case occurs, the workers in the Room will coldly signal this fact, cease their work, and throw the whole job through the OUT window. The workers never tire, never make a mistake, and perform each step of the work in a few millionths of a second. They can be instructed to store almost any quantity of information needed for reference, and they can type out the results of their work very neatly at the rate of several hundred lines per minute. They can serve several customers simultaneously, by special arrangement, without ever becoming confused or irritated. If the reader can think of the Room as the inside of an intricate electronic device, if he can visualize the workers as its components, and if he understands that every statement that begins with the word "never" is wrong, he now has some notion of what a high-speed electronic digital computer can do.

The computer is the heart of electronic data processing (EDP, an abbreviation used throughout this book), which in turn is now viewed by our most insightful educational leaders as a necessary tool in advancing theory, research, and practice in education. In subsequent pages, we inquire into the present status of EDP in information systems in education, analyze some of the problems and issues involved, and present recommendations for research and development. The focus is on elementary and secondary schools with only occasional reference to higher education. But first we take a quick look at the use of computer technology in other complex human endeavors.

Computer Applications in Military Affairs, Business, Industry, and Science

Acceptance of the high-speed digital computer, unlike that of many other great technical achievements, has been remarkably favorable in business, industry, science, and especially in national defense. In 1964 over $4 billion was budgeted for procurement of computer equipment, and an additional $2 billion was spent for programming and related software aspects of this equipment. There were at least 16,000 major computer installations in the nation during that year and 7,000 more on order. Approximately 1,250 of these were in use by the federal government (including the Defense Department and the Atomic Energy Commission), compared with 730 as recently as 1961. No doubt all these figures will appear puny a decade from now.

Computers, with their associated information processing systems, are essential to all space activities and to modern electronic warfare and are becoming an important tool in the development of national defense strategy. Only a computer can calculate swiftly enough to analyze the data from a satellite or to provide flight guidance for a rocket. Computer-centered command and control systems enable commanders to deploy strategic bombers, launch missiles, and provide early warning of an impending enemy attack. The global logistics and inventory systems of the armed forces could not function without computers. The resulting human responsibility for telling the machines the "right" things and the technical responsibility for foolproof response are at once frightening and overwhelming.

In industry, computer technology has had a tremendous impact on the improvement of production methods and on the science of management. Modern chemical plants and petroleum refineries are controlled by computers. In banks, insurance companies, large department stores, and most corporations that require large amounts of record-keeping, the computer has eliminated repetitive tasks and saved millions of dollars by company-wide integration of such functions as purchasing, inventory control, and scheduling.

Computer technology is exerting its influence on the scientific community. Scholars working in physics, optics, chemistry, engineering, psychology, economics, and other fields are using sophisticated computer analysis in research programs that, in turn, often produce totally new techniques and achievements. Even the humanist, for whom the machine must often be an anathema, sees in the computer possibilities not only for enhancing his research but also for advancing the dignity of man.

Before World War II, the only digital computers in use were analogue computers, desk calculators, and very slow mechanical switchbased computers. Military demonstrations of computer versatility and the scientific requirements of the space age have accelerated the growth of the computer industry. Following World War II, electronic computers were built at several centers, including Princeton University, MIT, the University of Pennsylvania, and the RAND Corporation. In 1951, the U.S. Bureau of the Census demonstrated the tremendous contribution of computers to government efficiency. In the middle 1950's, with the development of reliable high-speed computer memories, large and economically feasible computers began to appear in great numbers. Since then, computers have evolved from relatively small machines with slow equipment to large machines with very fast memories that perform work in millionths of a second and sophisticated information input and output equipment able to perform many operations at reasonable cost. The unit cost of computation has decreased by a factor of at least ten with each succeeding generation of computers.

Today, most computer installations operate in the plants and offices of several thousand corporations where they have yet to be employed in tasks that approach the full power of the instruments. So far, applications of the computer have tended to arise from the specific problems considered most pressing to management. Today the machine is largely being used to automate business functions and procedures previously done by manual

6

methods, since it is usually relatively easy to rationalize the cost of repetitive operations now being conducted by large numbers of clerical workers. Routine data processing involves preparing payrolls, recording and sorting bank checks, billing, analyzing personnel and financial data, and performing a wide variety of calculations.

But, now that the practicality of routine business applications has been demonstrated, more and more corporations are moving toward broader uses of computer technology. As a consequence of automating even a routine record-keeping process, the functions of an organization may change substantially. It may prove uneconomical to do only the present work when the computer system can do so much more. The information being processed may be found to have convenient additional and parallel uses. Sometimes new practices emerge to transcend previous ones. The anticipated installation of a computer forces users to think more precisely about what they want to do. Objectives must be carefully analyzed and specified in exact terms before the computer can be programmed. Computerization of a business function thus improves understanding of the process and reveals better ways for a corporation to conduct its operations, thereby increasing the likelihood of consolidating and integrating various functions. The computer can also yield entirely new types of information that will stimulate the development of new conceptual patterns within which business activity may be carried on. Finally, computer systems have now been developed that can be used as the central part of a communication network involving a number of widely dispersed elements of a business enterprise. Centralization of control and more effective management are facilitated since events are reported as they happen.

Another value of the computer is the increased capability it gives to business managers. More rapid and accurate assessment of complex environmental data permits better understanding of changing relationships among data so that circumstances can be controlled as they are developing. The computer can also help industrial executives through simulation techniques—using models of the enterprise based on past experience—to predict the results of policy changes. Many business and industrial operations, as well as complex social systems, can now be simulated in a computer for investigating decision-making processes. These techniques have increasingly been applied to management problems. One simulation program, using a minute of computer time, has been able to represent abstractly the operation of an entire business over a period of four hundred weeks. The company's operating data are fed into the computer, which evaluates several alternative decisions about finance, personnel, product scheduling, and other operating variables. From these evaluations, management chooses the most effective alternative according to the established criteria. But, of course, *men* must formulate the criteria and the alternatives.

Computers, by providing timely, relevant, and accurate facts, allow managers to rely less on intuition and more on systematic analysis; managers can thus use their time and imagination more creatively. Long-range planning, the development of new products, and the formulation of improved financial and public relations policies can now be given more attention.

The utility of the computer and its associated information processing systems depends on the ingenuity of the user. At present, a universally accepted classification of computer usage simply does not exist. The most successful users have clearly been those on the alert for new possibilities, even while the machines were being employed profitably only on routine tasks. Nonetheless, if the future of most of the fields now being computerized were sketched in by the few men most qualified to envision it, it would undoubtedly be scarcely recognizable even to today's most forward-looking executives.

Uncertainty about the future and mystery surrounding the computer itself have bred a measure of stress and insecurity, especially among mid-career personnel: "What, specifically, does it mean for me? Am I soon to be replaced?" They particularly fear replacement not by flesh-and-blood competitors they can understand, but by incomprehensible, inscrutable antagonists of seemingly limitless, indefatigable power. They also fear that the newly created need to specify their present functions for computer

8

programming may reveal their long-overlooked obsolescence. "Must I embark on a period of retraining, and will I be able to measure up?"

Even the poetic visions of a workless tomorrow with all sharing in electronically produced abundance is not necessarily everyone's Bali Ha'i. The recent upswing in "moonlighting" by workers is not fully explained by the desire for more money. Time on our hands can mean psychological trouble on our hands, and thus shortened hours compel us into a second job. Most of us have not yet found purposeful human work in a first or even a second job—though not necessarily because of the nature of the job or, for that matter, in our much-revered but naggingly unsatisfying leisure. Without such work, hope dies and the human spirit withers.[1]

These are clearly the critical problems of a rising generation and the generations to follow, growing up with and assuming as their birthright an increasingly mechanized legacy. The education future generations will receive must be profoundly different from the education we have known and know today. What should be the ends and means of this education? Will educators be able to grasp the possibilities and probabilities of the future and mold schools even reasonably appropriate to the challenge? What will be the role of computer-based information systems in these schools? Such questions loom large in an uncertain future.

Computer Technology
and the Changing American School

Next to national defense, education is the largest single enterprise in the United States. In 1965, expenditures for all levels of public education, including capital outlay, reached approximately $35 billion. The nation's schools and colleges enrolled one fourth of

---

[1] For a provocative distinction between labor and work and the implications of our failure to distinguish between them (and for many other related dilemmas), see Hannah Arendt, *The Human Condition* (Chicago: University of Chicago Press, 1958).

our population. With millions of people and billions of dollars to be accounted for, the American educational enterprise appears ripe for what computers can so uniquely do.

Information problems—ranging from problems of collecting, storing, communicating, retrieving, and displaying information to problems of receiving, learning, and using information—are woven throughout the fabric of educational processes. Teacher, administrator, research and guidance worker, business manager, board member—all are very directly concerned with transmission and utilization of information. Information is grist for computers.

National attention is now focused on the strategic importance of education. At home there are problems of economic growth, prejudice and racial unrest, even poverty and unemployment; abroad, a dozen hot spots call for continuous vigilance; beyond, outer space beckons us. Our educational institutions are expected to produce personnel capable of meeting our myriad exigencies today and tomorrow and of somehow leading the way to a better, calmer way of life. The past decade has witnessed pressure on our schools of a kind and intensity not experienced before. It is the nature of American schools to respond to a variety of appeals—and respond they have with a host of changes, both peripheral and fundamental. Let us examine briefly some of the forces thrust upon American education, some of the values underlying it, and some of the responses of a changing school.

VALUES AND FORCES

American education has been guided by the following ideals: education is for *all* Americans; education is designed to develop individuals to their full potential; education enables the individual to act intelligently; education contributes to the solution of virtually all social problems; education can never come too late; education opens up the largest number of roads to the good life. These ideals never go unquestioned, but they survive and, in fact, appear to strengthen their appeal in the face of adversity. The armor of those who war against them shines brightly for only brief interludes.

But, in recent years educators have been forced to interpret the significance of a bewildering array of forces and relevant conditions. Neither their meaning nor appropriate educational responses are readily apparent. Mathematic and scientific illiteracy among high school graduates, glaringly revealed during World War II, elicited post-war concern in the scholarly community and, with the launching of Sputnik in 1957, stirred large segments of the public. The explosion of knowledge has been and will continue to be much more than sheer exponential accumulation: knowledge is not simply piling up—awesome though the continuing expansion may be—but is constantly being recast into fresh constructs through man's never-ending inquiry.

Recently there has been a marked crumbling of the values that, although questioned, have provided a core of beliefs from generation to generation. Increasing numbers of persons are applying to the realm of values a hard-headed rationalism that assumes that nothing is to be accepted without question. Persons who take this view stand in conflict with those who regard certain time-tested beliefs as immutable, as a set of givens. These differences in viewpoint appear side by side each day on the editorial pages of most newspapers, and the tensions are sharply revealed in politics, government, economic affairs, and education.

Education itself is now granted a prominence and a role unprecedented in American life. Statistics as of 1965 reveal that poverty prevails in two out of every three families whose heads have completed less than nine years of formal schooling; they reveal that in the last decade jobs for high school graduates rose by 40 percent while jobs for those who failed to complete high school dropped by 10 percent. Because of the relationship between job opportunity and mobility, the quality of schooling in one section of the country is seen as directly relevant to the welfare of the nation as a whole.

We expect education to play a major—if not *the* major—role in eradicating crime and poverty, in assuring the good life for an increasingly large portion of the world's population, in raising the level of political responsibility, in expanding the nation's

11

economy, in purifying our streams and the air we breathe, and ultimately in assuring peace. We expect to bring education to everyone—as much as each person can use with profit to himself and mankind—without losing sight of the individual and each individual's uniqueness.[2]

We probably expect too much of education; certainly we expect too much of formal schooling. Schooling does not guarantee rationality or virtue or goodwill toward neighbors, even in those who partake of it extensively. Education does not by itself solve economic problems, remove racial inequalities, or ease world tensions. But education prepares the ground, we think, for enlightened human action.

As education in America has expanded quantitatively, the concept of education for all has become more inclusive and is increasingly compounded by our expanding insight into the startling and challenging realities of individual differences. Education for all includes education for the average, the gifted, the mentally retarded, the emotionally and physically handicapped, and the environmentally disadvantaged. Just as soon as neglect of some specific group is identified, immediate concern is evidenced and proposals are developed to take care of this group. Just as it is important to develop all Americans, so it is important to develop all their abilities. When science and mathematics were at last receiving their due attention, ears were turned to the appeals for art and music. Educators have no one-sided concern about the individual, nor have they fixed time limits for education. Programs for foreign-speaking citizens-to-be, easy admission from one level of education into another, and gargantuan provisions for adult education are all examples.

Schools must respond to exploding knowledge, science and technology, urbanization, and population growth; to the very cry for more and better education; to new insights into those who are

[2] For a succinct summary of contemporary forces, central values, and a program of action for American education, see John W. Gardner, "National Goals in Education," *Goals for Americans* (Englewood Cliffs, N.J.: Prentice-Hall, Spectrum, 1960), pp. 81–100.

to be educated; and to increased understanding of education itself. The responses of educators have not yet been adequate, especially for our social problems; they probably never will be. But some of them are imaginative and impressive.[3]

CURRICULUM REFORM

A massive curriculum reform movement is underway in response to international tensions and competition in space, the knowledge explosion, general dissatisfaction with school programs of the 1930's and 1940's, and various other interacting forces.[4] There are now many new configurations in the alphabet soup of educational groups and organizations: BSCS (Biological Sciences Curriculum Study), CHEMS (Chemical Education Materials Study), SMSG (School Mathematics Study Group), PSSC (Physical Science Study Committee), and so on. Each of these groups—and many others—has produced an instructional materials package comprising textbooks, supplementary reading material, workbooks, laboratory experiments and manuals, teachers manuals, films, and filmstrips. Underlying each package is an assumption about how the curriculum should be organized, which attempts to cope with the fact that expansion in knowledge has far outstripped the capacity of men to encompass it. Joseph Schwab has stated the knowledge problem dramatically:

At the present tempo of research in the western world, I would estimate the duration of a revisionary cycle in a median science to be on the order of fifteen years. Thus a body of knowledge acquired in the conventional way by a graduate of 1960 is likely to be largely inadequate by 1968 and, by 1975, as obsolete as notions of body humours, the ether, or the impenetrable atom.[5]

---

[3] For an analysis of the interplay between school and society during the past quarter of a century, see *The Changing American School,* Sixty-fifth Yearbook of the National Society for the Study of Education, Part II (Chicago: University of Chicago Press, 1966).

[4] For a summary and analysis, see John I. Goodlad and associates, *The Changing School Curriculum* (New York: Fund for the Advancement of Education, 1966).

[5] "Inquiry, the Science Teacher and the Educator," *The School Review,* Vol. 68, No. 2 (Summer, 1960), p. 180.

If the "conventional way" of acquiring knowledge no longer suffices, new ways must be found. The curricular assumption clearly evident in new mathematics and sciences curricula (which more than others were spawned by new knowledge) is that acquisition is best facilitated when learning is arranged so as to emphasize basic concepts, fundamental principles, and key modes of inquiry that compose the "structure" of the field.[6]

The approach calls for identifying these fundamental organizing elements and arranging curricular specifics in the most meaningful sequences. To date, a trial-and-error process of checking and adjusting to student responses has predominated, with the computer playing a role only in a very few projects that have proceeded more systematically. So far, the current curriculum reform movement is, in general, simply an implementation of important but largely untested assumptions. But, when programs seek experimentally to relate individual patterns of concept formation with subject-matter modules assumed to be logically derived, EDP techniques should prove indispensable.

PROGRAMMED INSTRUCTION

Closely aligned with certain assumptions underlying present curriculum reform, on one hand, and computer technology, on the other, is the advent of programmed instruction. The demands of programming force the programmer to come rigorously to terms with his subject matter and to be precise about the changes he is trying to induce in his students. According to B. F. Skinner,[7] the student in turn becomes actively involved in the teaching as well as the learning process.

Programmed instruction is in part a response to the challenge of providing for individual differences among learners. Should large numbers of good programs ever become available—and

[6] See G. W. Ford and Lawrence Pugno, eds., *The Structure of Knowledge and the Curriculum* (Chicago: Rand McNally, 1964) and Stanley Elam, ed., *Education and the Structure of Knowledge* (Chicago: Rand McNally, 1964).

[7] "Teaching Machines," *Science,* Vol. 128, No. 3330 (October 24, 1958), p. 969.

the lack of them and the difficulty of writing good ones together, currently, constitute a formidable bottleneck—students will be able to work successfully and competently by themselves for portions of their time, to select courses that would not otherwise be available, to make up missed work, and to strengthen diagnosed weaknesses. According to one theory, programmed instruction minimizes or even eliminates student differences that pertain to their actual ability to progress through a planned sequence: "If the learning program is successful, it insures positive transfer from lower to higher level learning sets for each individual learner, and thereby reduces individual differences in achievement of all subordinate learning sets in the hierarchy." [8] Presumably, then, when students become derailed, there are gaps in the sequence that should be filled with more subordinate learning sets. By carefully observing student performance, the programmer systematically refines the sequence until it is virtually foolproof. This theory raises questions of more than passing significance about the kinds of human learning that can be reduced to programmed sequences.

The systematic refinement of programs is of particular relevance in any discussion of EDP. Scanning the performance feedbacks of even small numbers of students on relatively short programs is a formidable task. But, when the size of the population is increased and diversified to include adequate samples of both sexes, various levels of tested intelligence, different past performances, and a range of socio-economic groups, this task quickly expands to astronomical proportions. Again, enter the ubiquitous computer, "The tireless serf already half a god. . . ."

The computer promises powers of observation in curriculum and instruction that may prove useful in theory-building, since controlled observation plays so significant a role both in formulating and in testing hypotheses. To date, our theories of instruction have been less than adequate, to say the least, and our theories of curriculum have been virtually nonexistent. Programmed teaching

[8] Robert M. Gagné *et al.,* "Factors in Acquiring Knowledge of a Mathematical Task," *Psychological Monographs: General and Applied,* Vol. 76, No. 7 (1962), p. 1.

machines, in turn linked to computers, may prove to be useful tools in fashioning more productive theoretical formulations.

SCHOOL ORGANIZATION

During the past decade, the graded structure and the one-teacher-per-class-per-grade organization of America's schools have been significantly modified. The relative success of recent attempts at modification, in direct contrast to earlier efforts, is probably due in large part to the viability of the alternatives proposed and being implemented. And, of course, we must never forget that these proposals have emerged in an era that demands alternatives. At other times, nongraded schools and team-teaching ventures might well have joined their predecessors—many of them close cousins —in history's vaults.

Nongrading, in concept, sweeps away the graded superstructure, graded content, graded textbooks, graded normative standards, graded children, graded teachers, graded expectations, and graded nomenclature to which we have long been accustomed. It is the fact that these accouterments of graded schools are so familiar that we fear and resist their departure. For graded schools, nongrading theoretically substitutes continuous pupil progress uninhibited by grade barriers; subject matter organized sequentially around fundamental concepts, principles, and generalizations; instructional materials gathered together for the task at hand and the varying abilities of the learners involved with it; criterion performance standards inherent in the learning task itself (excellence is determined from actual performance, not by comparisons with others); alternative classroom placements for learners based on pupil diagnoses and individual expectations for students; and still other provisions.

Team teaching casts aside the traditional, one-teacher-per-grade-per-subject concept of teacher use, together with our monolithic deployment of teaching talent. Instead of 30 pupils in a self-contained classroom with one teacher for all subjects or in a departmentalized plan with one teacher for each subject, visualize 75, 100, or 150 students supervised by a team of teachers and teacher aides, deployed into instructional groups of various sizes and space provisions appropriate to these groups. The teaching team functions under a leader and delineates staff functions according to the needs of students, the abilities of teaching personnel, and the demands of the tasks. A considerable portion of time goes to pupil diagnosis, counseling, and scheduling.

Many schools in the United States carry the nongraded label.[9] But none has fully achieved what has been envisioned for nongrading. Similarly, team teaching and various modified cooperative teaching plans are well enough established in theory and practice to have spawned a sizable body of publications.[10] But visions of what might be intoxicate the brain while practice lags far behind. This gulf is largely due to the need for reform in all those factors on which nongrading and team teaching depend: curriculum, materials, testing, teacher education, and information processing. Conversely, implementation of reform in these phenomena awaits the creation of flexible school structures such as nongrading and team teaching. Innovation occurs on a broken front, but, for the full possibilities of innovations to be seen and acted upon, education must be viewed all of a piece.

One way of viewing the consequences of interrelated decisions before they are made is to simulate a variety of possible answers— in essence, to anticipate and imitate the operation of a school or school system into which certain changes have been or are to be introduced. The variables and the possible relationships among them are too many to be manipulated manually or in the mind of one person. The computer has clearly demonstrated imitative propensities in other fields—particularly in commercial airline activities and in missiles programs—and is entering increasingly into the simulation of educational maneuvers.

Removing the traditional school structure that has largely dictated certain decisions about students imposes increased responsibility upon teachers. Expanding the range of learning opportunities available to students—as in team teaching, for example—also

[9] See Stuart S. Dean, "Nongraded Schools," *Education Briefs* (Washington, D.C.: Division of Elementary and Secondary Education, July 1964).
[10] See John Herbert, *Team Teaching, A Working Bibliography*, Horace Mann–Lincoln Institute of School Experimentation (New York: Bureau of Publications, Teachers College, Columbia University, 1964).

creates new teaching demands. Teachers must now diagnose each student, determine the best possible class placement, and subsequently relate student abilities and programs in a productive pattern. Suddenly there is urgent need for new information not days or weeks from now but here at the time and place of decision-making. The effects of these decisions must be subsequently observed and recorded. We have scarcely begun to realize the problem, let alone conceptualize the data needed and devise ways of obtaining them. The computer will undoubtedly be central to our solutions.

INSTRUCTIONAL MATERIALS

School principals report that what publishers produce for school use, particularly textbooks, is the most powerful determinant of what students actually study.[11] Staffs of the various curriculum reform projects are very sensitive to the preparation and production of instructional materials; most of the $15 million in annual National Science Foundation support for curriculum reform is spent on this aspect. Every conceivable audio-visual approach to the learning senses is employed.

A quiet revolution in the organization and use of instructional materials is taking place. In the past (and still today) energetic teachers wrote, telephoned, traveled, begged, borrowed, and probably stole in their zeal to assemble a wide assortment of materials calculated to titillate the interest of even the most incorrigible ten o'clock scholars. One teacher education course at a well-known university concentrated on the preparation of a bottomless box of teaching aids. Tired teachers, however, contented themselves with textbooks and workbooks—and perhaps a film on Friday afternoon. Goodness knows, the school library, if one existed, did not offer much.

The teacher's dream is to be able to "call up" at will photographs, paintings, books, pamphlets, objects, films, filmstrips, records, or even animals or people. Enlightened librarians function with this ideal in mind. The classroom comes into the library and

[11] *The Principals Look at the Schools,* Project on the Instructional Program of the Public Schools (Washington, D.C.: National Education Association, 1962), p. 23.

18

the library goes into the classroom. In some new school layouts, the boundaries between the two are scarcely distinguishable visually; other new buildings are often planned around the library, with special attention directed to the to-and-from flow of the student body. What appears to be of central significance in student learning has at last become central in at least some educational planning.

This concept of materials use and organization—the most appropriate teaching aid for the task at hand and a controlling pattern for all the instructional materials—suggests EDP systems. In a vast and complex materials system, there are millions of items and countless combinations for assembling them. Even in relatively small systems, the possible combinations stagger the imagination. Manual processing techniques simply cannot do the job.

THE EDUCATION OF TEACHERS

Computer technology potentially enters the education of teachers in two major ways: first, in the management of the teacher education enterprise; second, in the education of personnel who grasp the significance of EDP for improving the educational enterprise. The changing character of American education has brought about a need for specialized personnel of many kinds. Team teaching in elementary schools has created a demand for subject-matter specialists at that level; nongrading requires personnel skilled in pupil diagnosis; programmed instruction requires programmers; greater emphasis on individualized programs creates demand for counselors; systematic approaches to the use of materials necessitate persons capable of bringing programs and materials together. These demands rule out conventional "mass" approaches to the preparation of teachers.

Furthermore, young people entering teacher education curricula today come from diverse backgrounds of education and experience. Many have worked as camp counselors, as assistants in cooperative nursery schools, and as hospital volunteers; and now comes the returned Peace Corps group. To run these future teachers through a production mill is to do violence to their individuality and to deprive the schools of special talents that might be honed

19

through individualized teacher education techniques. The problem is to bring backgrounds, interests, goals, and selected curricular activities into effective juxtaposition so that the needs of the individuals and the needs of the schools are met simultaneously. Teachers of teachers must devise the conceptual schemes; computers stand ready to process the data.

As for the second potential role of EDP in teacher education, there is now a gap between conceptions of schooling and of computer science. Because educators do not understand the computer and what it might be able to do for them, they think in terms of manual data processing. They scarcely dream of what might be facilitated were EDP techniques introduced. The computer scientist, in turn, is not sufficiently aware of school problems to see beyond the use of EDP for relatively routine tasks. Into this knowledge gap must step educators who can think productively of an educational future in which the computer serves appropriately. We speak to the preparation of such persons in later chapters.

Educational Problems Today and Tomorrow

The continued use of antiquated information processing procedures in the face of the growing size and complexity of American education constitutes a gross anachronism. Education is in large measure an information processing system. The right data at the right moment give teachers and administrators the edge they need for making calculated rather than uninformed decisions. Wisdom and information are a powerful team. Computers can provide the information; educators must provide the wisdom. We have seen that American education today involves billions of dollars and millions of people, changing curricula, new patterns of school organization, more effective means of supplying and using materials, and diverse decisions about instruction and administration. The problems range from counting things and people to matching things and people; from studying things and people to simulating relationships among things and people; from making

20

decisions about things and people to innovating with things and people; from a concern over deliberately controlling things and people to speculating about things and people. EDP plays a potentially powerful but presently too-neglected role in all these.

We have seen, too, that the present and potential uses of EDP in education range from relatively simple but quantitatively significant tasks of storage and retrieval of masses of raw data to tasks calling for involved decisions and research. Table 1 depicts

TABLE 1

Problems in Education Appropriate
for Electronic Data Processing

LEVEL 1 *Raw data*	LEVEL 2 *Relationships among data*	LEVEL 3 *Decisions and research*
GENERAL POLICY AND ADMINISTRATION		
Codification and systemization of school laws, sources of funds, health and safety regulations, etc.	Effect of new policies on school health and safety records	Study of relationships between policies and teacher and student effectiveness
Results of polls on citizen expectation for schools	Patterns of relationships between sub-publics and types of expectations for schools	
	Relationships among types of administrative problems and processes used in decision-making	Conceptualization of possible new relationships and simulation of the consequences of effecting these relationships administratively

21

TABLE 1 *(Continued)*

LEVEL 1 *Raw data*	LEVEL 2 *Relationships among data*	LEVEL 3 *Decisions and research*
FACULTY, STAFF AND STUDENTS		
Comprehensive inventories of teacher backgrounds	Relationships between age, institution attended, credentials, etc., and teacher retention in the system	
Long-term collections of data on student achievement, attendance, health, dropout, etc.	Relationships between school achievement and student health	Prediction of student achievement in school from longitudinal data, followed by deliberate manipulation of the environment and analysis of the consequences
BUDGET AND FINANCIAL SUPPORT		
Statistics on school costs broken into budgeted categories		
Maintenance of assessed evaluation statistics and data pertaining to proportion of district income spent on edution tion	Relationships between financial support and various evidences of school productivity	Decisions pertaining to school bond referendums and building construction in relation to alternative predictions of population growth and financial support, together with calculations pertaining to how much new industry will be attracted by new and better schools

TABLE 1 *(Continued)*

LEVEL 1 *Raw data*	LEVEL 2 *Relationships among data*	LEVEL 3 *Decisions and research*
FACILITIES		
Cost statistics on all aspects of school construction and maintenance	Relationships between costs of various types of construction and costs of maintenance	Manipulation of facilities to test hypotheses growing out of observations at level 2
CURRICULUM, INSTRUCTION, AND MATERIALS		
Number of students in various patterns of curriculum	Relationships between student high school curricula and later academic and work careers	
Student responses on programmed lessons and courses	Relationships between responses and age, IQ, past achievement, etc.	Study of student learning styles and various provisions for them, such as different sizes and types of groups
Storage and retrieval of data on student assignment to individual instruction, large groups, small groups, etc.	Relationships between student assignment and various aspects of student success	Manipulation of the instructional-grouping environment to test hypotheses growing out of observations at level 2

the range of tasks for which EDP procedures might be appropriate. Listed from top to bottom are five realms of educational activity; across the top are three levels of conceptual complexity. Level 1 calls for processing large quantities of data, level 2 for drawing out relationships among categories of data, level 3 for formulating

23

research designs and making major decisions. Setting up the data processing system presumably demands cognition higher at level 3 than at level 1. The categories could be extended and arranged differently; they serve simply to conceptualize a range of possible uses for EDP in education.

The educational activities listed under level 1 parallel a long list of activities in business, industry, and the military that are now commonly being managed by computers. Consequently, one finds few new problems here in seeking to apply EDP techniques in the field of education. Similarly, the processes implied under level 2 are now routine in many enterprises. There are far fewer models for level 3 tasks, and so we can anticipate the emergence of new approaches, some of which will contribute to fields other than education, as educators make use of EDP in coping with this category.

Level 2 reveals a rather interesting phenomenon. Thousands of theses, dissertations, and research studies in education and psychology concern themselves almost exclusively with patterns of relationships between socio-economic factors and success in school, between student and teacher values, between creativity and intelligence, between school system salaries and teacher mobility, and on and on. Such studies often involve careful selection of criteria and preparation of instruments. In the past, they have also involved painstaking hand checking of tests of significance. These statistical analyses, formerly requiring months of such labor, can now be processed in minutes of computer time. It is even more significant, however, that now hundreds of possible interrelationships of data—each one of which might well have been appropriate for a master's thesis a few years ago—can be explored equally quickly.

This capability of the computer points to the conclusion that an entire class of research studies formerly considered fair game for the graduate student are now simply not worth his time. It is questionable that they ever challenged the intellect appropriately, but the answers required tedious work, and graduate students were ready slaves. The dangers are in equating such efforts with scholarship and in condoning countless hours of hand processing of data because of our allegiance to a misplaced conception of appropriate human work.

Graduate schools must now involve their students in research studies requiring a higher level of conceptualization to be certain both that human talent is appropriately challenged and that problems of significance become better understood. With the computer performing the labor, analyses of relationships among data will very often be conducted as routine preparation for research requiring entirely new conceptions of hypothesized relationships. This will more often than not be team research, involving professors as principal investigators assisted by graduate students with cooperative as well as individual functions to perform. It is hoped that students who ultimately join the academic ranks from such programs will stimulate more significant educational research than we have witnessed in the past.

This analysis of the research category could be extended to all aspects of Table 1. Such an analysis would reveal that the educational enterprise stands to profit enormously from the more efficient information processing that is already affecting business, industry, science, and the military. The problems involved appear not to be unique, especially at levels 1 and 2. In all realms of human endeavor, the challenge is to relate automation effectively to the purposes of man, not to subvert the purposes of man for the sake of automation.

Conclusion

To assign top priority to education—for people of all ages as the means of preventing human disasters is to express once again the characteristically American confidence, perhaps over-confidence, in education. In any case, to perform effectively the roles so often assigned to it, education must become more efficient. We turn, therefore, to analysis of present applications of computers and to information processing systems in education with the hope of shedding further light on what is required for the future.

2

Electronic
Data Processing
in Education:
Present Developments and
Technical Aspects

The Scope of Present Developments in Education

Significant pioneering work in applying electronic data processing procedures to education is now under way, and interest among educators and applications in schools are increasing rapidly. Among those who have already experienced the benefits of automated systems in education, the significant questions are not whether EDP methods are to be used but rather when, where, and how they are to be used most effectively.

Nonetheless, the applications of computer technology in education have lagged far behind those in business, science, and government. The computer sciences have so far had only a limited impact on education, and automated information systems are still the exception rather than the rule. Surveys indicate that only about

300 of the 2,100 colleges and universities and about the same number of the 30,000 public school districts in the United States now own, rent, or use electronic accounting machine (EAM) equipment or computers.

Most educators still use relatively primitive techniques for processing the wide variety of information required in the daily operation of schools. Using papers, pencils, and typewriters, they produce a vast number and variety of records and reports pertaining to students, teachers, budgets, and accounting transactions. Endless hours and professional energies are consumed in routine clerical work that could easily be taken over by a computer. Some attention is now being given to computer applications in instruction, research, school administration, guidance, and related elements of the educational program. However, these are so limited in number that they must be considered experimental.

Until recently, comparatively few educators were even aware of the nature and scope of computer and information system applications in education. Those educators who were generally lacked the necessary technical knowledge to introduce EDP systems into their own school districts. This unfortunate situation is now changing rapidly. Increasing numbers of educators are recognizing the computer's potential, even though few possess the understanding necessary to use computers effectively.

This chapter seeks to develop this understanding and provide a perspective for the discussion in Chapter 3 of present computer applications in education. The following two sections summarize the factors hampering or promoting the growth of these applications; the bulk of the chapter then discusses some technical and procedural aspects of EDP in education.

FACTORS HAMPERING COMPUTER TECHNOLOGY

What factors are involved in the comparatively slow growth of computer applications in education? Some are psychological and are similar to those found in the early applications of EDP in business and industry. Many educational practitioners do not relish the prospect of automation, just as a significant number of business and industrial personnel did not and, frequently, still do not.

The unknown world of the computer sciences tends to threaten their security.

In education, however, there are inhibiting factors that have not affected other enterprises to the same degree. Education is above all an activity conducted by and for humans. Furthermore, it is considered one of the professions. Connotations of the concepts "human" and "professional" are such that automation of any part of education appears to be somehow degrading and suspiciously dehumanizing. This viewpoint of course overlooks the mass of routine to be taken care of in so large and complex an enterprise as well as the potentially humanizing effects of easing this burden through automation.

There are economic deterrents, too. Educators are faced with the realistic problem of maintaining modern educational programs on fairly constant incomes in relation to the number of pupils served. Limited school budgets are already stretched just to keep pace with constantly increasing student enrollments. It is extremely difficult to justify large expenditures of money for new computer or EAM equipment unless significant cost savings and increases in efficiency can be readily demonstrated. Pressures for the purchase of language laboratory equipment, audio-visual materials, or other relatively well accepted instructional devices, for new building programs, and for annual increases in faculty salaries tend to have priority in school budgets and serve to crowd out exploratory programs involving EDP applications.

There is also a serious lack of knowledge on the part of educators about the power and potential of computer systems for improving educational programs. Probably the most important reason for the slow diffusion of computer applications in education is the poor dissemination of results already being achieved by successful installations. School personnel in general do not know what computers and data processing systems can do for them. However, from the experience gained in the military, business, and science fields, it seems likely that growth in understanding and an increasing knowledge of existing installations soon will break down resistance in education. Utilization of EDP systems should then increase rapidly.

Many computer specialists feel strongly, and with good reason, that every program of general education should include material designed to acquaint all citizens with what computers can and cannot do. In a rapidly moving technological society such a step might even be considered an urgent requirement; the need of the data processing industry for EDP specialists is well known.

Within education itself there are two needs that are not being met adequately. In order to increase the rate of EDP applications in education, it is necessary to train educators to understand and use available computer resources. All educators need to know more about EDP and its place in education, and they need enough specific information to cooperate intelligently with the system they will be involved with. The second problem is that there is a great shortage of persons qualified to design, establish, and operate educational data processing systems in school districts. Those now in the field generally learned while on the job. As of the winter of 1964, no institution of higher learning offered a complete course of study for professional specialization in educational data processing. A few colleges offer a single course or a summer workshop, and computer programming or EAM operations are taught as separate disciplines in hundreds of schools and colleges.

What is lacking is a curriculum as thorough as that for the school administrator, the psychometrist, the teacher, or even the educational research worker. The scarcity of opportunities to study educational data processing continues to be a major obstacle to utilizing the resources of computer technology in education. What little we can learn from occasional short courses or workshops indicates, principally, the inadequacy of such measures. In the opinion of those who have taught such courses or who have been responsible for training EDP personnel, internships in operating systems are needed. Internship training should include thorough instruction in computer programming, EAM processes, systems analysis, facility planning, statistics and research methodology, management methods, and business operation. Lacking such instruction or courses of study, the best that interested educators can do at present is pick up a course here and there, read the small but growing literature of the field, and try to obtain on-the-job experience.

FACTORS PROMOTING COMPUTER TECHNOLOGY

Despite the obstacles, however, compelling forces at work in education today are precipitating the predicted growth of EDP in schools. Foremost among these are the seemingly endless expansion in enrollment and the inadequate supplies of qualified instructional personnel. Administrators are looking to EDP for the release of teachers from routine clerical and accounting duties. The very existence of these myriad chores spotlights the potentiality of automation. And so many different groups want data: taxpayers, newspapers, school boards, state departments of education, the U.S. Office of Education, legislators, researchers. For each of millions of students, hundreds of items pertaining to health, achievement, attendance, interests, and abilities are generated, processed, recorded, copied, filed, evaluated, and indexed. Information formerly not even gathered is now deemed essential for planning curricula, evaluating instruction, counseling students, and administering schools.

Public pressures for increased productivity, reduced costs, and greater efficiency in education in the space age are factors conducive to growth in EDP. The pace of technological progress and information growth will continue rather than diminish. Education must be responsive to the environment in which it operates and to which it contributes. If schools are to provide graduates attuned to the society in which they live, much more emphasis must be placed on efficiency and high quality in the educational process. Data processing methods promise to provide these attributes. If applications of computer technology continue to expand in scope, there is every reason to assume that significant improvements in educational productivity will result.

We saw in Chapter 1 that a host of recent changes in American education places new demands on information processing. For the improvement of curricula, rapid feedback from trial use with thousands of students is essential. For the refinements of nongrad-

31

ing and team teaching, data pertaining to pupil diagnoses are required. For efficient instructional use of diversified materials, automated cataloging and retrieving systems are mandatory. These innovations call for computers; computers in turn facilitate such innovations.

Associations and Agencies Promoting
Electronic Data Processing

Prior to 1961, there were no professional associations primarily concerned with the special problems of educational data processing systems. Educators interested in data processing and data processing specialists interested in education could join the Association for Computing Machinery, the Machine Accountants Association, the Association of School Business Officials, and similar groups concerned primarily with computer hardware and software or with accounting machine applications. National and regional conventions of educational and psychological associations—for example, the American Psychological Association (usually for the benefit of measurement specialists), the American Educational Research Association, the Psychometric Society, and the American Association of School Administrators—occasionally scheduled special interest meetings on educational data processing.

In 1961, a small group of educational data processing specialists in California, meeting with the California Educational Research Association, discovered sufficient interest in data processing to warrant holding a trial statewide convention which met in Los Angeles in November 1961. It was obvious from the attendance of more than one hundred and thirty people that many educators recognized the need for a professional association; hence the California Educational Data Processing Association (CEDPA) was formally founded in the spring of 1962. It was the first such association in the nation and is still one of the largest. Three regional CEDPA subgroups meet in the intervals between annual conventions. Professional associations for educational data systems have also been formed in Colorado, Florida, New York, Oregon, and Texas.

In the fall of 1962, motivated by similar concerns at the national level, a small group of educators from state departments of education, universities, and large school systems founded the Association for Educational Data Systems (AEDS). This organization held its first annual convention in Washington, D.C., in May 1963. The *AEDS Bulletin,* published monthly, carries news of professional interest to AEDS members.

Founded originally at Chicago Teachers College North, the *Educational Data Processing Newsletter* appeared in 1960–61 with a very limited initial subscription list. By 1962, the operation of the *Newsletter* had become too burdensome to remain a personal effort, and the voluntary staff of the *Newsletter* established the Educational Systems Corporation (ESC) as a nonprofit educational corporation in California. Representing both national and local organizations on its board of directors, ESC now also publishes a *Journal* and has initiated a series of monographs.

The National Science Teachers Association sponsors the Project on Information Processing (PIP) and publishes the *PIP Newsletter,* which covers the instructional uses of computers in science and mathematics.

In recent years, the Department of Audio-Visual Instruction of the National Education Association has sponsored a Technological Development Project that has produced literature on school information systems and computer-based instructional systems. The Computer Oriented Mathematics Project of the National Council of Teachers of Mathematics is actively exploring the role of computers in secondary school mathematics.

Several other associations also have an interest in some major aspect of educational data processing. The Association of School Business Officials led the way in introducing more efficient methods in the business management of schools. The Business Equipment Manufacturers Association, through special subcommittees working jointly with the American Standards Association, represents the educational interests of the major equipment manufacturers. The Data Processing Management Association has established a program of examinations and certification in an effort to raise the professional standards of those engaged in data processing work.

Special interest groups of college and university users of particular computer systems have been very active in recent years. The College and University Systems Exchange (CAUSE) and the Machine Records Conference, like other user groups, seek to exchange technical and professional materials and experience. Members of user groups meet periodically for detailed work on specific technical problems.

The need for national coordination of the educational data processing interests of professional educational associations became apparent at the time AEDS was formed. Representatives of major associations, most of whom have their headquarters at the National Education Association building in Washington, D.C., established a Council for Educational Data Systems in the fall of 1962. Still informal in organization, it was to provide a means for communicating with educators about developments in educational data systems. In addition, the Council was established to speak for the educational profession when it needs to represent itself to EDP specialists and manufacturers concerned with technology and systems operations.

State departments of education have recognized that educational data systems are of increasing concern to the states and that it is desirable to coordinate state efforts in the national interest; the Council of Chief State School Officers (CCSSO) therefore established a Commission on Educational Data Systems (CEDS) in 1963. The Commission was charged with the responsibility for conducting studies, formulating recommendations, and planning for development on behalf of the departments of education in the fifty states. A nine-man executive committee represents the CEDS membership between the annual meetings of the Commission and of the CCSSO.

Finally, the U.S. Office of Education has subsidized the use of modern data processing in state education agencies under several titles of the National Defense Education Act of 1958 and the Cooperative Research Program. From 1959 to 1963, under Title

X of the NDEA, the federal government responded to requests from state education agencies with grants of more than $5 million to be used on a matching basis for the improvement of statistical services in these agencies. The funds have facilitated significant growth in the use of automated data processing at the state level. Of the fifty-five states and territories covered by the NDEA, only thirteen were making use of EDP equipment in September 1958, whereas fifty-one of these education agencies were using such equipment in 1964. Moreover, a large number of states have plans to take advantage of opportunities for developing EDP programs under Title V of the Elementary and Secondary Education Act of 1965.

Technical and Procedural Aspects of Electronic Data Processing Systems

In this book, we have attempted to avoid unduly technical or obscure terms. Before examining the specific applications of computers and information systems in education, however, we must clarify our use of certain EDP terms and discuss the capabilities and limitations of EDP equipment. The balance of this chapter deals with the following technical and procedural aspects: (1) hardware design and use, (2) software design and use, (3) the use of facilities, and (4) the intersystem flow of information.

HARDWARE DESIGN AND USE

EDP equipment, or "hardware," as it is commonly called, has developed so recently, so rapidly, and with such diversity that this chapter deals with it only in a very general way. (See Appendix C for several comprehensive texts that describe various types of computing equipment and their use.) In general, hardware of major interest in education falls into three categories: simple punched card equipment, also called unit record or electronic accounting machines (EAM), digital computers, and accessories. With the exception of scoring machines for the mass processing of test answer sheets, few if any of the available hardware systems have been designed for the particular needs of educators. Instead, educators have adapted present hardware to their own needs.

EAM equipment can record data on cards (sometimes called Holerith cards) in the form of punched holes and can sort, collate, compare, copy, print from, and tabulate these cards. The EAM is a unit record installation; that is, each card must be acted upon before another is considered. The computer differs from the EAM unit in many ways: the computer operates at much higher speeds and therefore the cost per unit of work is low; it permits greater flexibility of control and processing—for instance, the computer can handle cards singly or can consider many cards before taking action on all or any of the data they represent; it provides its own data storage (in addition to what is "stored" in the input medium itself); and it can alter its own control and processing procedures (called programs) according to varying circumstances. EAM devices, as their name suggests, were primarily designed for accounting work; computers were designed for scientific and mathematic use, although they have also proved useful in accounting and statistical work.

Simple punched card equipment was in use before 1900 in the United States and Europe, but it became widely available only after World War I. Until the end of World War II, information processing machines consisted principally of EAM units. Even today, most educational data processing systems employ EAM units with punched cards to replace paper-and-pencil processing. After information has been transcribed onto punched cards, data processing assistance is then obtained from electrically operated machines that were originally designed to perform accounting functions in business and industry. These machines are now being used to perform similar clerical tasks in schools and are extremely useful in processing large volumes of data.

An EAM installation may consist of several pieces of equipment. The keypunch places holes in the cards, and it may also print along their upper edges. The sorter arranges punched cards in order and counts or selects them. The reproducer is used principally to copy all or part of the contents of the cards or is sometimes used as an output device for other machines. The collator is used to merge or select cards, to match sets of cards, to check sequences, and to do other editing work. The tabulator is a printing device, capable of printing entire lines of type at rates varying from fifty to one hundred and fifty lines per minute; most tabulators are equipped with simple logical and arithmetic units that permit some selective treatment of the cards and simple operations with the data punched in them. The interpreter prints prepunched data directly on cards for ease in handling.

An EAM, though simple compared to a computer, is a complex of many functional units that are independently controlled. For example, the units within an accounting machine control the movement of punched cards; "read" punched holes; recognize special cards and the boundaries between groups of cards; add, subtract, and compare numerical data; and print information. Only by making appropriate electrical connections can the user combine these units into a special-purpose machine capable of performing a specific task. Some connections are made so frequently that external switches are provided, but it is impossible for switches to be installed for the millions of potential connections; for these a control panel, commonly known as a plug board, is provided. Though simple in structure, the control panel serves as the nerve center of the machine. It is a frame for holding the contact ends of the wires in fixed positions so that thousands of wires may be clamped to the machine to complete appropriate electrical circuits. EAM units are simple to operate, but control functions for them are tedious and complex to design, and they lack flexibility. Their cost varies, depending on their speed and capacity, but they are within the reach of all but the smallest or most impoverished school districts. Many EAM units are necessary or useful as accessories to computers.

Simple EAM units, however, have definite limitations. It is the high-speed electronic computer, the center of advanced information system technology, that is receiving the most attention from educators. Large scale programmed computers, with their vast speed, storage capacity, accuracy, and versatility, are now demonstrating utility in almost every information processing aspect of education.

37

The cost and performance of computers are directly affected by the type and number of specialized units in any particular system. Computers vary in size and capacity from simple devices that may be carried about by hand and plugged into any ordinary wall outlet to very large computer installations involving many interconnected EAM units with extensive air conditioning and special power sources. Some of them require thousands of square feet of floor space. The earliest digital computers, of which few remain, were electromechanical—that is, they used wheels, levers, and rods activated by electric power. The first truly electronic computers used vacuum tubes and hence generated a large amount of heat. Today, the most widely applied computers use cooler solid-state devices such as transistors and therefore require less air conditioning.

The computer may use punched cards for its input or output functions but it is distinguished from punched card machines principally because its processes are controlled by an internal *program* —a sequential set of instructions that the computer stores and then acts upon according to a predetermined logic that has been fed into it by a computer programmer. Since these instructions are coded as numbers, they may be modified by the computer itself in precisely controlled ways. Computer programs must be so written as to take account of every foreseeable contingency. Any administrative rule that can be specified can be programmed into an EDP system, but it remains the prerogative of the educator to make those inexplicable but intuitively correct decisions he alone can make. Computers cannot make decisions that the educator has not already instructed the computer to make.

The "heart" of a computer is its logical control and processing unit. At any moment, input may come from a manual keyboard or typewriter, a punched card or punched paper tape reader, a magnetic tape unit, another computer, or an optical reading device. Output units may be of the same type, except that a card punch would be used rather than a card reader, and visual or auditory display devices might be added. Storage devices include spinning drums or discs, magnetic tapes, electronic tubes, and ferrite cores (small rings of metal enmeshed in a matrix of connecting wires). Newer ways of storing data—for example, methods that exploit the molecular structure of special compounds—are now under development.

Accessory computer devices include card-handling equipment (trays, trucks, and racks), storage equipment (for cards, documents, control panels, magnetic tapes, and wires for the panels), and paper-handling devices (for feeding and collating forms, separating and decollating them, and printing vertical lines on tables). These accessory devices are usually purchased, whereas most EAM units and computers are rented or leased.

Test scoring machines constitute a special class of accessory computing devices. The most widely used scoring machine, the IBM-805, is actually a computer. It compares marks on a test answer sheet with a key pattern, measures the resistance to electric current of marks properly made, and translates the results in the movements of a needle on a visible dial, which the operator notes and records. In the last decade, several optical systems have been devised. These use variations in light intensity caused by the presence or absence of marks in prespecified positions. The largest scoring machines (such as those at the Measurement Research Center of the University of Iowa and at the Educational Testing Service in Princeton, New Jersey) permit automatic feeding and handling of the input documents and produce output that can be punched in cards for later printing or can be transmitted directly to magnetic tape or the storage system of a computer. As document-reading devices are perfected to read and translate handwritten letters and numbers, additional uses will be found for these large special-purpose machines—for example, taking attendance, reporting grades, analyzing questionnaires, and recording work or performance.

The educator contemplating the development of a data processing installation in his own school district might well ask, "What configuration of equipment should we choose?" The kind and quantity of equipment used in education and the practices employed vary widely. Moreover, examination of current school practices seems to reveal no consistent correlations between particular configurations and the size of the population to be served, the geographic location, or the type of EDP application required. Local school districts employ equipment ranging from a simple EAM installation renting for approximately $350 per month to small computer systems renting for approximately $4,000 per month. Some relatively small districts are using one or more computers in a wide variety of applications, while some large districts are still using EAM equipment. Many districts begin by using a service bureau and then progress to their own installations, adding different applications as they gain experience.

Most data processing installations adapt to changing needs and capacities by expansion; few installations maintain the same configurations for more than two years, and even fewer do so for more than three years. One criterion for choosing data processing equipment is therefore to ask what configurations of equipment are readily adaptable to *future* needs. This is a very practical question because school administrators must constantly face the economic considerations involved in the rapidly advancing EDP field. Computers and associated equipment on the market today may be outdated a few years from now, and an expensive initial investment in the new technology may cause unnecessary financial problems over an extended time period.

In evaluating the adaptability of a particular installation, we must therefore consider its ability to expand through minimally disruptive change—that is, change that necessitates a small loss in previous software and increases flexibility. The move from EAM to the computer is a special exception; it is often extremely disruptive. However, disruption may be tolerated because of the very great increase in capability and efficiency effected through a computer installation.

Growth in the power of a small installation comes customarily through the addition of a different type of machine. Will the new configuration be powerful for its size? Will it have fundamental, inherent weaknesses from having been expanded without adequate foresight? Like its predecessor, the new configuration has to be chosen primarily to assure performance of the tasks that justify its purchase. Unfortunately, these future problems can be only dimly foreseen. The wider is the potential range of uses, the sounder the investment is likely to be. Even the man who has to dig a posthole may be much wiser to buy a shovel—a *general purpose* digging tool—than to buy a posthole digger.

Fortunately, we may safely follow a clear path through this maze of unforeseeable problems, assuming there are no freakish local circumstances. For each size of small installations in EDP— that is, for each number of equipment pieces in an installation— there is a popular configuration. For instance, Table 2 shows that

TABLE 2

Popular Punched Card Equipment Configurations
(Computer Installations Not Included)

Number of different types of equipment installed	Number of respondents using that number of pieces	Popular equipment configuration	Number of respondents using config- uration	Percent of respond- ents using configu- ration
1	4	Keypunch	3	75
2	5	Above, plus sorter	5	100
3	21	Above, plus accounting machine	16	76
4	11	Above, plus reproducer	8	73
5	26	Above, plus collator	16	62
6	16	Above, plus interpreter	8	50
7	15	Above, plus test scoring machine	7	47

SOURCE: Data reported in L. R. Reed, "Data Processing Systems," May 1963, privately reproduced (by hectograph). Of 288 known educational data processing centers, 225 were queried (including all the centers outside California) and 165 responses were elicited. Because of incomplete data, however, only 98 respondents are presented in column 2.

five EDP centers indicated they had two pieces of equipment in their installations; the two pieces used by all five centers were the keypunch and the sorter. Expansion of the installation is accomplished by adding the next larger single machine to the original configuration; this new configuration then stands ready for equally simple expansion to the next larger size of installation. As Table 2 suggests, the most popular sequence of expansion seems to be to begin with the keypunch and then add successively the sorter, the accounting machine, the reproducer, the collator, and the interpreter. Beyond this rather complete installation, the path becomes dimmer. The next preferred machine, the test scoring machine, can be added at any time. Centers electing any of the smaller configurations can add to it at any time and be assured that many educational applications can be performed.

A computer is added to the configuration usually because of increasing work loads that cannot be met by an existing machine group, but such an addition is a very serious step. Not only does cost mount sharply, but some elements of the EAM configuration (for example, the keypunch) have to be retained for support. The true test of the necessity for a computer is to ask this question: What will the computer permit us to do that we cannot now do either with comparable efficiency or merely by increasing the number of hours of EAM utilization?

SOFTWARE DESIGN AND USE

In the world of EDP technology, the term hardware has a fairly well understood meaning: it designates machines, computers, and accessory devices. The term software, however, is a source of confusion. It is sometimes loosely used to designate "all that is not hardware." We use the term in this book to designate computer programs (whether listed on paper, punched in cards, or recorded on magnetic tape) and their documentation, written descriptions of manual and machine procedures, input and output forms and formats, coding systems and layouts, and drawings or other representations of wiring and information flow.

The development of software is often considered to be as costly as that of hardware. Unlike capital equipment, however, computer programs and procedure descriptions are easily reproduced. Hence the development cost of software can be shared, with consequent savings to all concerned, given expedient modes of communication and exchange.

A punched card installation is sufficiently different from a computer installation to warrant a separate software discussion for each.

Software for the Punched Card Installation

The guidance and control of data through a punched card installation has been a major problem because costly, continuing personnel time is required. The staff of such an installation thus has a large responsibility for job description, recruitment, training, and retraining. Many centers have underestimated their personnel needs and have consequently suffered woefully from insufficient and inefficient machine utilization—from inadequate documentation, expensive job pick-up (transfer of job from operator to operator), and difficulty in training new personnel. Such installations become excessively dependent on the individual, who must carry much of the necessary software knowledge in his head.

Data processing installations perform a variety of jobs, many of which are rarely done the same way on successive occasions, most recurring only on a long term cycle. A punched card installation therefore demands a large number of variously wired plug boards. The number of plug boards needed is usually underestimated by the salesman attempting to install an EDP system at an acceptable cost and is often underestimated even by the supervisor, who may be familiar only with the conventional commercial installation. The Richmond, California, school installation has over 50 IBM-407 plug boards, but this number of boards is unusually high; most EAM installations struggle along with from 10 to 20 boards. Punched card installations with an inadequate number of plug boards lose much time in tearing down and rewiring boards for jobs recurring infrequently, and much of this time involves expensive use of personnel.

Punched card guidance and control may be categorized as (1) procedures concerned primarily with the sequence and details of manipulating punched card decks and (2) plug boards. The first area has to be, and generally is, better documented. Operators with little training must be able to pick up a recurring job previously performed only once or twice under close supervision. They therefore require explicit written instructions that can be omitted only by means of expensive, continual supervision. Plug boards are rarely well documented. There is often little internal need for documentation, and boards for recurring jobs are generally wired permanently. The very expensive job of diagramming is sometimes deemed an extravagance.

Diagrams or other notations are needed, however, for boards that must be rewired. The decision to tear down a board involves an evaluation of the difficulty of rewiring, including the preparation of the necessary documentation and an estimate of the probabilities of having to rewire within given intervals of time. The crude diagrams used internally are rarely of any value to an outsider. Generally color-coded, they do not reproduce well. Idiosyncratically notated, they are largely meaningless to anyone other than the author. Hence, there is very little transmittal of sophisticated plug board software from installation to installation. Similarly, many procedures are worthless without documentation of the basic plug boards. Obscure journals occasionally publish an article that includes a board diagram, and manufacturers have published some monographs with board diagrams. Several volumes of *Educational Research Forum Proceedings* represented an early attempt by IBM to meet needs in this area. The difficulties of developing widely usable software at the punched card level results in a very slow rate of "lore diffusion," forcing each installation to be its own research and development center. Many ingenious but now outmoded early software developments were never well disseminated. An example is Educational Testing Service's factor analysis techniques using a conventional IBM tabulator; another is an elaborate punched card method of assigning secondary students to class sections in Huntington Beach, California. Indeed, the possibilities of using the tabulator to compute percentiles or sums of squares and cross-products for correlation calculations were generally unknown, simply because these so-called progressive digiting techniques were never widely understood. Only a few installations had tabulator plug boards for producing graphs and scattergrams. The only communality we can be sure of finding is the wealth of unwritten experience in the minds and fingers of the operators and supervisors trained on the job in commercial installations.

Sophisticated punched card software is now being replaced by the computer just as surely as metal tools replaced highly developed bone and stone tools. Elaborate and often highly ingenious early punched card methods were justifiable only until more economical computer facilities became available.

Software for the Computer Installation

With the wide availability of the computer came a substantial change in information processing. Basic control need no longer rest in an expensive wired plug board that is hard to store and difficult to reproduce. Control functions can now be replaced by an inexpensive, easily stored reproducible program on punched cards, paper tape, or magnetic tape. Procedures describing elaborate card handling are obviated by the manipulation of the data within the computer itself, entirely under the control of a self-monitoring program. A small computer installation can generally go into operation immediately, using borrowed programs in compatible input formats.

The programs themselves are written in one of several languages that permit relatively easy local modifications. It is now possible for a few centers or institutions—such as the New England Educational Data Systems at Harvard University (NEEDS) or the California Research and Development Center at Sacramento—to be the source of many programs used throughout the country.[1] It is indeed fortunate that the relative ease of transmittal and exchange of software makes it possible for educators in one school district to draw on the resources of another, because software is the most serious and expensive obstacle in the development of a computer installation. Computers can assist more than half the time in the writing of their own programs, but the ratio of program development time to operation time is still forbidding, especially in the early stages of computer utilization.

[1] For more details concerning these programs, see Chapter 3 and Appendix B.

The cost of software development and maintenance affects the total operating cost of a computer installation. These costs in turn are very much affected by the quality and quantity of software provided by the manufacturer, who generally provides the compilers that make possible the use of the variants in the major programming languages. One may expect the manufacturer eventually to offer a library of utility programs and subroutines that greatly simplify programming. There is also a system of maintaining an annotated catalog of programs available through a cooperating organization of users. Some manufacturers managed to get a substantial head start in the software area by installing computers in the universities and developing strong cooperative groups of users. Other manufacturers have met the need by making very heavy expenditures in their own software development departments.

One serious problem, however, is the short supply of programming personnel, especially in locations remote from large metropolitan centers. In even shorter supply are programmers who understand educational statistics, educational data processing, educational jargon, and human factors. Lacking such personnel, it is necessary to have on the EDP center staff an educator who understands computer technology sufficiently well to define an educational problem in terms the programmer can handle. Fortunately, the work of good programmers, when well-documented, can be exchanged and disseminated at low cost.

Input and Output Forms

Most forms used to transmit information may be divided into two large classes: internal and external. Internal forms are used either by the EDP system staff for its own work or as the input to a machine. For example, a punched card to be handled only by experienced EDP personnel does not need a form printed on it at all; the operator can look at a card layout guide and interpret readily what the holes signify. If an EDP system uses punched cards on which the codes appear, it does so for convenience and for checking purposes.

External forms are designed either to collect or to display

information. For example, if a teacher is to make marks on a document that will later be mechanically processed, and if these marks are made with reference to particular students, the form must show the identity of the students and the exact nature of the entries to be made. In other words, to reduce the chance of erroneous use, forms used to collect information must be uncluttered, unambiguous, and readable. The other major class of external forms, those that display information to parents, pupils, and school personnel, include report cards, test results, attendance summaries, transcripts of records, test data profiles, and correlation scattergrams. Experience shows us that such output documents must emphasize clarity of presentation. Secondary emphasis is given to esthetic value and to such mundane matters as whether the size of the documents fits a particular envelope or filing drawer.

The design of internal forms is usually left to the discretion of the EDP staff. The design of external forms is usually accomplished, under the best conditions, by a combined team of EDP specialists and those who will process the forms. In most cases, the EDP specialist begins with the old forms from a manual system and designs several alternative forms for machine processing. He then works with the educator in selecting, modifying, and combining the elements.

Veteran EDP specialists in school systems report that it is very valuable to consult all school personnel who have any concern with forms. The specialist may design a perfectly logical and usable form all by himself, but the educator usually has new ideas he may have waited a long time to advance. Furthermore, it is good practice to involve the educator in all possible phases of EDP system design, since the forms that will be used for input and output of information constitute the principal contact the educator will have with the new system.

One feature of EDP systems in schools that has received comment is the multiplicity of forms designed for similar purposes. Specialists visiting a variety of school systems may collect a hundred different report card forms from a hundred different districts; most of them differ only in very small details or in arrangement. In the early history of the Cooperative Plan for

47

Guidance and Admission (CPGA) in Georgia, analysis of these proliferating forms showed that more than 90 percent of the items were identical in purpose and content. Disagreements were often matters of trivia: whether to say "boy/girl" or "male/female," or whether to state age in years and months or only in months. Real disagreements about content pertain to local concerns that could be accommodated in widely used forms by permitting optional use of certain items.

Large numbers of different forms designed for similar purposes are not only confusing but costly. New forms usually involve design, plate-engraving, and composition charges. In California, some school districts that agreed on common use of certain card forms found they could reduce costs by mass purchasing through a single agency.

Nonetheless, it seems certain that the practice of local control in school districts will mean long time delays before all school systems accept the desirability of surrendering local interest to common regulation. In the meantime, since the additional cost involved is not so great, there seems little reason to balk local initiative until agreements can be reached. In the opinion of most EDP practitioners, it is unfortunate that general agreement cannot be reached, but meanwhile school systems must move ahead. The achievement of local objectives is probably much more important than are minor gains in widespread efficiency. Again, as in the case of intersystem cooperation, the answer is compatibility rather than uniformity.

THE USE OF FACILITIES

The first question an educator must consider when contemplating design of a facility for data processing is this: What is the extent and nature of its utilization? This question will be asked repeatedly in varying forms as the system and the installation evolve together. Even though there are some subtle issues involved that do not make immediate sense to school accountants and budget-watching school officials, school administrators and EDP technologists agree that everyone concerned with facility utilization should have at least one common purpose: full and effective utilization. For instance, a process requiring eight hours of EAM work might be done on a computer in eight minutes. But it is obviously not economical to acquire a computer if it is to be used only eight minutes a day.

The term "full utilization" is not self-evident, however, because utilization cannot be judged entirely by the percentage of time equipment is in use. This is an extremely important point that school officials interested in getting started with EDP should be aware of while facing questions of economy. For example, in one county installation, an IBM collator was used only 20 percent of the available day-shift time. Word was passed down to discontinue its rental. Analysis of the forseeable consequences of such an apparent economy move showed that the work done by the collator in that 20 percent period would have required the manual labor of two clerks at roughly five times the cost of the monthly rental of the collator.

The history of most EDP and computer installations shows that a piece of equipment usually does not receive full utilization in the early stages. Gradually, however, as work expands and the machine is integrated with the system, a high capacity point is reached. If the load increases, as it always seems to, another point is reached at which the inability of the machine to accept a heavier load seriously affects other processes in the system. For example, if a tabulator running at the speed of 50 lines per minute cannot produce desired reports within a necessary time limit, even by running the device all the time, a faster one must be obtained. Of course, a faster tabulator, perhaps one operating at one hundred and fifty lines a minute, may complete the required work without being utilized to full capacity, and it will sit idle part of the day. But not for long. The record shows few examples of failure by EDP personnel to find new work for more efficient machines.

Most facilities expand at a rate slower than that of their load. In almost every operational installation today, one finds that faster, larger, or more powerful devices are on order, usually for delivery at a much later date. Such orders were usually placed only after the overload on the existing system had already become painfully evident to everyone except the administrator responsible for approving acquisition of the new—usually additional or more expensive—device. Fortunately, EDP personnel have become adept at planning their work around such difficulties. They use external service bureau facilities; they scrounge, borrow, or buy time from other installations during off hours or periods of diminished load; they work overtime or run the machines into the night and on weekends. They may even quietly place orders or letters of intent to order long before official approval has been obtained. In some cases, equipment ordered today may not be deliverable for many months, sometimes more than a year. Hence, seasoned EDP specialists report that they place orders in the hope of subsequent approval in time to accept delivery—and in the knowledge that, if worst comes to worst, delivery may be delayed or cancelled.

There are several factors to weigh in considering the use of a service bureau or other external facilities as an alternative or supplement to one's own equipment. The easiest tasks to process on external equipment are the initial and terminal ones. For example, large keypunching jobs can be farmed out, and final printing of a report can be done remotely or at the point of use. It is obviously cheaper to use equipment on a part-time basis if one needs it only part of the time. As soon as the cost of using service bureau equipment approaches the cost of having one's own equipment, the switch may be made. However, if the external equipment is remotely located, or if it can be used only at inconvenient hours, cost estimates must include the personnel time required for travel or for overtime assignment. Moreover, the entire EDP system may be affected by delays in processing or by insufficient opportunity to control the procedure or respond to unexpected emergencies or variations. For example, one school district that used mark-sense cards for quarterly course reports did not have its own mark-sense device. After minor clerical editing, the incoming cards had to be boxed and then transported to an external facility that had a mark-sense device. This procedure required the school staff to delay the next steps in processing the course reports until mark-sensing was completed on all the cards. In this case, the school district's use of its own mark-sense equipment would have facilitated the entire course-reporting process. When the district eventually acquired its own mark-sense device, the work proceeded more smoothly simply because the staff could work on other tasks or on other machines while the thousands of cards ground their way through the mark-sensing process. The elimination of delays in packing, travel, repacking, and return were additional bonuses for the district.

As the use of an EDP facility increases in volume, experience shows that it also generally increases in scope. That is, a greater variety of work is done for more persons and departments. This means that a facility sooner or later faces the problem of whether to operate on an "open shop" basis. Ordinarily EDP equipment is initially acquired by a business office or a research department to do its own work. Later, as time and opportunity permit, it begins to do work for other departments. Soon these other departments come to depend on such aid, and finally there comes a day when both payroll and report cards must be processed at the same time. Priority will generally be given to the needs of the proprietor or to the department with the greatest "political influence." Wise scheduling, of course, can prevent such emergencies in most cases.

However, in all mature installations with which we are familiar, the issue eventually has to be faced: How and under whom is the EDP facility to be managed for the good of all departments? Also, how much decentralization is effective? The experience of EDP specialists has shown that, with few exceptions, the administration of EDP systems should be placed close to the top executive. In a school system, directors of information processing and EDP services who report directly to the superintendent appear to have the most effective, widely admired, and accepted systems. The value of an EDP facility declines roughly as the square of its distance from the user increases. If it is too difficult or complicated to obtain access to the equipment or to the services, they generally will not be used to full advantage.

The EDP administrator should be a member of an advisory group that sets priorities on the general nature of work to be done and departments to be served, plans and reviews the budget for the system, and evaluates the effectiveness of services provided. The difference between an accepted system and a rejected one depends heavily on the extent to which consumers and users of the service are included in the development of policy and program as well as in the evolution of those portions of procedures and regulations which impinge directly on the educational staff. The operation of the EDP system seems most successful when it is made a part of the institution as a whole rather than the sole domain of a major branch of the institution.

THE INTERSYSTEM FLOW OF INFORMATION

An ideal of any farsighted system designer is to integrate all parts of the system in a logical and efficient pattern of static and moving parts. As EDP methods begin to be adopted in education, anomalies appear that disappoint and baffle the system designers. For example, students transferring from other districts appear with transcripts made out originally by a tabulating machine from punched card records. The contents of the transcripts must be repunched for use in the local EDP system. Or reports sent from local school districts to state departments of education are carefully typed from records printed by a high-speed computer on magnetic tape, requiring the staff of the state department to repunch the data for use in its own equipment.

There are many obstacles to be overcome in developing procedures that permit one EDP system to communicate with another, either directly, by wire or microwave, or indirectly, through machine-readable (sometimes called machine-sensible) documents.[2] Devices that permit functional connections between computers or between input-output devices and computers make teleprocessing technically possible. A teleprocessing unit permits the user to dial a distant computer installation just as if he were placing a telephone call and to obtain access to a computer, using regular telephone lines. Information stored on magnetic tape may be communicated either by sending the actual tape or a copy of

[2] That is, documents prepared in a "language" the computer readily manipulates.

it, or by attaching a tape-handling machine to a teleprocessing unit. Transcripts of records can be communicated to a remote location on documents read by optical scanners that convert the contents to a form immediately usable by the computer. The cost of teleprocessing is reasonable; the devices are becoming in-- creasingly available and efficient; and the equipment of various manufacturers is beginning to reflect a growing interest in compatibility.

Can one logically expect, then, to find educators making use of this technology? With minor exceptions, the answer is "no." The exceptions involve portions of well-understood processes. For example, when a pupil takes a standardized test and indicates his answers on a machine-scorable answer sheet which is then sent to some distant center for scoring, there is minimal intersystem teleprocessing. In the Richmond, California, EDP center, teachers use punched cards to report absences to a central office, which uses the cards to make mechanical records. In Georgia and some other states, optically scanned forms are prepared manually so that high school transcripts of college applicants can be processed at a center in Princeton, New Jersey. The Measurement Research Center in Iowa processes millions of test answer sheets and returns results to schools on either punched cards or magnetic tapes.

These few instances of intersystem efficiency of communication, however, are less impressive than the gap between the available technology and the use being made of it. Some of the major reasons for believing that such intersystem transmittal will be slow to emerge are (1) the magnetic tapes used on one manufacturer's equipment may not be usable on another's; (2) formats (on punched cards and on magnetic tapes), terminology, and systems of coding differ from one school district to the next, and between schools and colleges; and (3) legal and administrative differences in attendance accounting definitions and procedures exist among all fifty states. An "A" may be worth 4 points in one system, 5 points in another, and 40 in still a third. Spanish 1 may be a one-semester course in one system and a one-year course in another. One district uses local norms, another national norms;

53

one uses percentiles, another IQ's, another mental ages, and yet another, grade-placements.

Not all intersystem information exchanges require telecommunication or the transmittal of machine-readable documents, and the use of central information systems need not bring all the information to the center itself. The best example of an information system with many remote "nerve endings" is the automated reservation system now used by airlines. Using a similar system, it may be possible eventually for a college to interrogate an applicant's high school without actually having the record in its own files. Much progress has been made by the College Scholarship Service, for example, which permits scholarship applicants to fill out a single statement of financial condition that is centrally edited and analyzed; it then furnishes information to a variety of potential grantors or colleges. Similarly, instead of taking several entrance examinations, applicants to College Entrance Examination Board member colleges take a single set of tests, which are centrally scored and processed; the results are then sent to any college or scholarship agency the applicant designates.

During the past several years, the U.S. Office of Education has taken steps to establish a Basic Educational Data System (BEDS), which begins by collecting a few simple facts about every certificated school employee in the nation. A state interested in comparing its teachers with those of a neighbor (or with the other forty-nine states) can thus have access to data of great potential value in the formulation of policy. Many states are expected to furnish social security numbers for BEDS to be used, in cooperation with the Social Security Administration, for additional studies. This arrangement permits intersystem data analysis without revealing the identity of any individual.

Although there are few examples of intersystem exchange, plans for such systems are widely discussed and are being studied in research, development, and service centers. As described in Chapter 3, NEEDS provides for cooperation between more than twenty school systems and a central service agency. In the near future, it will be possible to transmit data about students from one NEEDS school to another as pupils change residence. Such transmittal is a reality in most large school systems in which an EDP system is centralized; that is, when a pupil moves from one school to another within the same school system, his record is altered to show the fact, but it remains in the central EDP data bank. In Sacramento, California, the Research and Development Center of the State Department of Education is devoting great effort to the development of systems in California and to the problem of exchanging data between schools and the Department of Education. In just a few years, most schools in California should be able to report results of the mandatory statewide testing program to the state agency in punched card form. Similarly, school systems in Florida that have EDP facilities are beginning to make reports to their state department of education in machine-readable form.

In the opinion of many EDP specialists, it may take a long time to develop intersystem exchange and transmittal to an effective level, but the results of such cooperative systems may well be among the most significant. It is here that the greatest potential for cost reduction may lie. And the accessibility of accurate data for states and for the nation as a whole, as a by-product of intersystem transmittal and exchange, may provide a sounder basis for the development of educational policies, programs, and legislation.

Conclusion

EDP is not an advanced art in the field of education. Primitive paper and pencil techniques still prevail for most educational information processing. Moreover, even the limited applications of computers in education merely mechanize routine procedures for storing and retrieving data pertaining to management and administration. The use of computers for innovations in curriculum and instruction constitutes a frontier being explored only at the research and experimental levels.

Since EDP has advanced so much further in other realms of

activity, one must conclude either that EDP methods cannot solve educational problems or that there is a tremendous lack of knowledge among educators about the potential of EDP. Clearly the former is not the case, although there are many problems of adaptation, particularly for software, and although it is difficult to anticipate future needs for hardware in education. Furthermore, the efficient, economical use of EDP calls for a close cooperation among school districts that has not hitherto been required. Nonetheless, the major obstacle to the advancement of EDP in education is the tremendous gap that exists between the technological development of EDP and the comprehension educators have of this great potential service. The next chapter examines some of the applications of computers and information systems now in operation or in experimental or research stages.

3

The State-of-the-Art:
Applications
of Computers
and Information Systems
in Education

Introduction

Electronic data processing methods in education now enter into a considerable range of activities. Well-designed, tested, and practical means exist for processing the usual data associated with business: budget, payroll, accounts payable and receivable, ledger accounts, property management and inventory, and tax rolls and assessments. In addition, a growing number of schools use EDP to handle pupil personnel data: census, registration, schedules, progress reports, transcripts, GPA and class rank reports, sectioning by abilities, medical and dental records, physical fitness and disability records, and test results. Employee personnel records are processed by EDP methods in many school systems. In a few states, teacher certification procedures are similarly processed. Research work is materially assisted by automatic processing, and the existence of machine records in many areas of school operation makes possible more economical and consistent evaluation and prediction of the effect of educational policies and procedures.

EDP methods have been used by state and regional associations and governmental units for a variety of management purposes. In one instance, legal opinions regarding school law are indexed on punched cards for easy cataloging and distribution, saving thousands of dollars in legal fees and obviating delays. In another, test answer sheets are processed for dozens of school districts too small to have their own EDP equipment; computers are used for scoring tests as well as for processing the results of testing. In one state, computers are used to make substantial improvements in the efficiency of school bus routing. In state education agencies, accounting procedures affecting local districts are now performed in minutes rather than weeks, with great savings in time and cost and with the dividend of permitting the comparison of different solutions by examining the results of alternative policies. Scheduling procedures—the assignment of pupils to sections according to a master schedule—can now be substantially mechanized. A wide range of applications may be found in local school districts, both large and small, in state EDP programs, and in regional projects that serve several states.

Until recently, almost all EDP applications had one common characteristic: they were an outgrowth of specific school-information handling problems that were considered most pressing by the school officials. The computer and electronic accounting machine equipment were used primarily to automate the general business and student accounting tasks previously done by manual methods. Furthermore, research and development in the field were aimed primarily at improving conventional data processing procedures. In this respect, the state-of-the-art of educational data processing has followed the pattern of growth identified earlier for business applications. Payrolls, budgets, pupil registration, attendance, school marks, achievement test data, and related matters are all logical extensions of computer experience in industry. Machines are programmed for schools in order to perform existing information processing functions, since it is relatively easy to justify the cost savings that result from the elimination or reduction of repetitive operations now being performed by clerical personnel. Within the past five years, however, research and development activities have increasingly focused on new methods of instruction, including developments in optical scanning devices, language translation machines, computer-assisted instruction, rapid document-retrieval systems, and computer models of school district operations.

This chapter first examines in broad outline the four main types of functions that computers and information systems perform in school operations. This general discussion is then followed by descriptions of selected EDP programs that illustrate these functional applications in detail and that also sketch some future possibilities for data processing in education.

Functional Areas of Computer Applications

EDP is already proving useful in four functional areas of educational program: *general business accounting*—the financial and property accounting of all school business; *student accounting*—the processing necessary to regulate and record student activities; *general administration*—the overall direction and control of students and employees according to policies and practices specified by local, district, state, and national educational systems; and *instructional programs*—the presentation to students of programmed curriculum materials and the rapid retrieval of documents and reports for instructional purposes.

GENERAL BUSINESS ACCOUNTING

California local school districts initiated EDP in a typical way. In reporting a statewide study of pupil personnel data processing in California, Alvin Grossman points out that many school districts began with payroll functions and proceeded to accounts payable.[1] After developing their business accounting, they began to consider student accounting. This sequence is often followed

[1] "A Report of a Study—Processing Pupil Personnel Data," California State Department of Education Bulletin, Vol. 31, No. 2 (March 1962).

because EDP applications in the business world already are developed and are readily adaptable to business accounting in school systems.

At the time of Grossman's survey, approximately 75 percent of the responding county and local school districts used their EDP equipment for one or more areas of school business accounting, including accounts payable, budget, cafeteria, cost analysis, equipment inventory, payroll, purchasing, retirement, and transportation.

One of the best illustrations of the state-of-the-art in school EDP business accounting is found in the Chicago public schools. Stanley R. Patton, Director of the Bureau of Data Processing for Chicago schools, reports that his data processing staff works on six major projects, three of which involve aspects of business accounting: (1) budget and finance, (2) personnel and payroll, and (3) materials.[2]

The IBM-305 Ramac system used by the Chicago schools provides monthly expenditure journal entries for the general ledger and produces a "status of accounts" report that depicts the financial condition of each school or administrative unit— information that was not available under the previous manual system. Plans for the expansion of EDP included revenue accounting; Patton anticipated that this service, added to the schools' expenditure accounting, would be able to provide complete journal ledger accounting and a detailed balance sheet shortly after the close of each month.

Personnel accounting (for example, records of hiring, managing, and reimbursing teachers and civil service employees) is also part of EDP operations in Chicago. Teacher payroll, now processed on a small computer, will eventually be processed on a large magnetic tape computer system.

The Materials Project for the Chicago schools encompasses supplies, transportation, communications, purchasing, maintenance and repair, property control, plant engineering, lunchrooms, and textbooks. The information needs of this project have been

[2] *Progress Report on Total Information Service* (Chicago: Bureau of Data Processing, Chicago Public Schools, May 1963).

studied, and an integrated plan has been prepared for EDP processing. Warehouse and supply catalogs have been codified and put into machine-readable form. Patton also reported that the supplies subsystem would determine what, when, how much, and where to stock. A further computer role is to produce the picking and packing lists for the warehouse according to delivery schedules and to issue stock reorders automatically as any item reaches its order point. This application of EDP technology to school business accounting was designed to reduce administrative and clerical costs so that a greater share of available funds could be applied to instruction.

STUDENT ACCOUNTING

Unlike school business accounting, student accounting procedures have had very little to draw upon from well-established commercial machine accounting. Furthermore, the variety of requirements from district to district has prevented rapid and widespread adoption of the successful procedures that have evolved. Consequently, there is considerable diversity, and independent developmental activities are conducted in many school districts across the country. Student accounting requires, for one thing, a substantially different kind of personnel from that needed for school business accounting. Imagination, verbal facility, and understanding of the educational process are characteristics of the successful systems designer in student accounting. Thorough grounding in machine accounting is a significant but less important asset.

Many universities were early users of punched card methods for maintaining student records. The concentration of many students under a single administration and the expenditure of relatively large sums of money per student probably effected an earlier introduction of such methods at universities. Also of significance was the relative ease with which procedures that required the intelligent cooperation of students could be used.

At the secondary school level, the first applications of electronic processes to student accounting were generally a later application of equipment that already had been justified for business office

61

applications. Los Angeles was using such methods in handling test data in the 1920's, and Pasadena was developing punched cards by 1942. In 1947, the Los Angeles district reported that, in addition to the handling of test data, the Accounting Machines Services Section was compiling reports on student accidents, work permits, absence, attendance, and movie permits.

Today, more sophisticated computer installations allow for more comprehensive student accounting services. For example, Broward County (Fort Lauderdale, Florida), in addition to attendance accounting and testing, reports provision of the following services: student schedules (by semester and year); teachers' schedules, class rolls, locator cards, welfare cards, attendance cards, and teachers' loads (all by semester); library labels (annually); student rosters (by semester and as required); teachers' grade audit sheets and report cards (every six weeks); permanent record labels (each semester and annually); and current and cumulative GPA reports (every six weeks, each semester, and annually). Under the same heading are locker assignments, bus rosters, ranking reports, graduation listings, assembly seat assignments, and grade distributions. At present, Broward County is also operating a pilot computer student scheduling program that provides class assignments for approximately 23,500 students in seven senior high schools and four junior high schools. Finally, computer programs operating in a Broward County junior college maintain records of many kinds for 2,100 students.

The technological problems of computer assistance in the assignment of students to conflict-free schedules have been solved to the extent that almost all high schools of over one thousand students could be aided substantially by available methods. Yet, comparatively few schools have tried them, largely because few educators have acquired the necessary skills for successful trials. As described later in this chapter, recent work at Stanford University, MIT, and the University of Pittsburgh indicates that operational computer systems for making the master schedule itself, together with diagnostic materials to evaluate curricular alternatives, will soon be available on much more than pilot or experimental bases. Maintenance of cumulative student files and abstracts of pupil data using magnetic discs is being explored at Palo Alto and has been tried at Ft. Lauderdale, using both discs and tape.

GENERAL ADMINISTRATION

Relatively little progress has been made in using EDP systems to improve general administrative practices in the schools. However, there are many EDP applications that can be of substantial assistance in solving school administration's most serious problems. EDP techniques can be applied readily in taking a census of school and preschool children within various school boundaries to determine projected school attendance, set up bus service boundaries, select the most suitable locations for new construction, and help school officials forecast needed facilities and services. Other potential EDP applications that would be invaluable include specifying bus routes under various safety constraints (such as a low number of railroad crossings) to determine bus and driver requirements; simulating master schedules of school construction to determine certain architectural specifications and faculty needs; and, at the state level, determining (in a matter of minutes) the cost effect of state aid formulas.

These administrative decisions are not entirely simplified, however, because new vistas are opened up that bring with them new problems. Some other decisions that could previously be easily ignored must now be faced. The very existence of computer technology removes critical impediments to the implementation of innovations such as modular scheduling, the nongraded school, and the coupling of team teaching with single-section courses. As a consequence, excuses for maintaining the status quo come less readily.

INSTRUCTIONAL PROGRAMS

The application of data processing technology to the functions of teachers, counselors, and librarians has been confined primarily to streamlining reporting procedures, accounting for and taking inventory of books, and scheduling classes. The time saved on these bookkeeping tasks allows librarians, teachers, and counselors to give more personal attention to students. Some school libraries have automated checkout and catalog searching procedures in combination with the production of periodic listings of new acquisitions. Improved efficiency and convenience for students have resulted.

Attention to computer-based teaching machines, document abstracting and retrieval systems, and computer-mediated business and economic games have remained the primary concern of researchers working in laboratories and field installations throughout the country. Perhaps because of this, a widespread trend toward the application of data processing technology to instructional functions has not yet developed. In recent years, however, several major universities, private research and development firms, and state departments of education have installed computer-linked typewriter input stations in classrooms and laboratories for faculty and student use. Among the more significant programs being developed for practical instructional applications are the following:

Western Reserve University

The University's Center for Documentation and Communication Research is recovering data and source articles for students and professionals in the fields of metallurgy, inorganic chemistry, physics, mechanical engineering, and medicine.

The Ohio State University [3]

At Columbus, Ohio, the University recently announced plans to install a computer-based instructional system involving two GE-636 time-sharing computers, eight small-scale GE-115 computers, and a number of display terminals. The displays will be located at strategic campus locations, including laboratories, classrooms, and selected faculty offices and research facilities.

[3] *Aviation Daily* (September 29, 1965), p. 169.

Stanford University [4]

Under a 1963 Carnegie Corporation grant, Stanford University designed, developed, and is now operating a computer-based laboratory for teaching and learning. The initial effort has been in developing elementary school mathematics programs under the direction of Professor Patrick Suppes, Chairman of the laboratory's executive committee. This research, conducted by the Stanford Institute for Mathematical Studies in the Social Sciences, is also supported by the Course Content Improvement Section of the National Science Foundation. Initially, twelve six-year-olds came daily for thirty minutes of individual work at computer terminals, where they received a complete mathematics curriculum under computer control. Analyses of their responses served to redesign the first-grade program for more general use.

The Stanford laboratory consists of six student stations. At each station is an IBM terminal displaying a microfilm image on which the student may respond with a light, a Philco cathode-ray tube (CRT) with an accompanying typewriter keyboard, and a Westinghouse audio system. The audio system provides random access to prerecorded messages. The student responds to lesson displays and the computer, in turn, scores his responses. The IBM microfilm devices store 256 pages per cell (4 pages per film clip, 64 clips per cell) and use 2 cells. The screen may be divided into 8 individually controlled sections. Answers may be by a light pen (when it touches the screen the coordinates of points touched are relayed to the computer) or by a keyboard.

The Stanford group feels that computer-based instruction can provide extensive accommodation to individual differences, unprecedented data recording and analysis, teacher relief from routine tasks, and systematic ordering of curriculum sequences. Plans for extensive cooperation with other centers for research on computer-based instruction are proceeding rapidly.

[4] "Computer-based Laboratory for Learning and Teaching," *Automated Education Letter,* Vol. 1, No. 1 (October 1965), pp. 17–18.

The University of California [5]

The University of California, Irvine, slated to become one of the larger links in the state's university system, recently announced its plans to participate in one of the most extensive computerized instructional experiments undertaken so far. This effort, a joint research project with IBM, should be significant as a model for developing computer-based instructional systems in colleges now faced with rapidly expanding student enrollments and new demands brought on by the information explosion.

Professors at UCI will assist in the project by helping to develop automated lessons to aid students in assuming responsibility for individual learning at their own pace. The initial UCI computer facility (IBM 1410-1440-1448) will provide for more than twenty students at a time, with remote typewriter-like consoles in the library, classrooms, laboratories, and dormitories. The computers will also facilitate an evaluation of each student's progress from entrance to graduation, budgeting, the ordering and cataloging of books for the library, and payroll processing and accounting functions. The faculty is being encouraged to develop imaginative new uses for the computers in instruction and research.

The Pennsylvania State University [6]

Faculty members at this institution are preparing courses in modern mathematics, cost accounting, audiology, and engineering economics for presentation to students by means of a computer. The system uses an IBM-7010 and an IBM-1410 computer configuration with remote IBM-1050 typewriter terminals. The main computer is located at the IBM Thomas J. Watson Research Center in Yorktown Heights, New York, and the typewriter terminals are located on the campus of Pennsylvania State Uni-

[5] *Ibid.*, p. 19.
[6] Harold E. Mitzel and Kenneth H. Wodtke, "The Development and Presentation of Four Different College Courses by Computer Teleprocessing," *Interim Report,* U.S. Office of Education–sponsored project. Title VII, Part B, NDEA Act of 1958 (University Park, Pa.: Computer-assisted Instruction Laboratory, College of Education, Pennsylvania State University, June 1965), p. 9.

versity. Transmission of information between the University terminals and the central computer takes place over long-distance telephone lines by means of teleprocessing. The instructional terminal (that is, the IBM-1050) consists essentially of a modified IBM Selectric typewriter which permits two-way communication between a student at Pennsylvania State and the computer at Yorktown Heights. The terminal also contains a random-access slide projector and tape recorder attachment. Course material can be presented to a student by typeouts, slides, or tape recordings. In answering a question or problem, the student types his answer at the terminal and relays it to the central computer. The computer then provides knowledge of the results to the student, remedial information, or the next problem.

Courses are prepared by means of an IBM-developed computer language known as *Coursewriter*. This language enables an author with a minimum of special training to include questions, problems, assignments, correct and incorrect answers, provisions for unanticipated answers, knowledge of results, and branches or alterations in sequence in his course. In addition, an author can employ a procedure known as Student Records, which will record and store all student errors and response times.

The System Development Corporation [7]

Long active in the development and application of computer-based instructional systems involving the Computer-based Laboratory for Automated School Systems (CLASS [8]), the System Development Corporation (SDC) of Santa Monica was recently awarded a National Science Foundation grant to develop a computer-based system designed to improve the teaching of statistics and the training of future research workers in education. Based on the latest developments in information processing and instructional technology, the system will employ computer time-sharing, natural language communication between user and computer, and programmed instruction. Initial design work will be conducted in the CLASS facility. Subsequently, the system

[7] *Southern California Industrial News* (November 1, 1965), p. 7.
[8] To be discussed later in this chapter.

67

will be installed in classrooms at the University of California, Los Angeles. Students studying the behavioral sciences will be taught how to use the computer and associated mathematical techniques as applied to the field of statistical inference.

UCLA students participating in the study will have access to a large computer installed at SDC headquarters by means of a time-sharing system developed by SDC that enables a large number of remote users, working on independent programs, to use the same computer simultaneously. The project will use a question-answering program developed at SDC that allows the student to write questions to the machine in English. It is believed that this program will rectify a common student complaint about computer-based instruction, which is that he cannot now ask the machine to explain why a particular statement was made or why certain answers are correct. In addition to using computer programs from a library of them, the student may also write his own program using a language called TINT. Developed by SDC, TINT employs an algebraic-like language that allows a student with no programming experience to readily acquire computer programming skills.

The Massachusetts Department of Education [9]

During the 1965 school year, five Massachusetts communities initiated a program to use computers in the classroom teaching of mathematics. Sponsored by the Massachusetts Department of Education under a grant from the Cooperative Research Program of the U.S. Office of Education, the project uses a network of six teletypewriter terminals connected to a Bolt, Beranek, and Newman (BBN) computer located in Cambridge, Massachusetts. The initial stages of the program include a six-week summer course at BBN to acquaint elementary and secondary school teachers with the computer equipment, the programming language, and system capabilities.

The above examples of computer-based instructional programs provide a cross-section of the work underway and a foretaste of much more to come. The potentialities for research into the

[9] *Electronic Data Processing Weekly* (August 30, 1965), p. 15.

learning process are enormous, and this research will inevitably place stringent demands on the behavioral sciences. Most other uses of the computer in education are relatively routine by comparison. At least some of the work planned or in progress promises to lay a solid base for a truly scientific diagnosis of the learner's progress and, subsequently, for educational prescription from a tested range of curricular alternatives.

Illustrations of Activities in Educational Data Processing

The following section provides representative examples of the resources now available in educational data processing and their present and future uses. The specific illustrations are grouped under three main areas of activity: (1) educational information systems currently in operation that illustrate many of the functional applications discussed in the preceding section, (2) research and experimental work to exploit the potential uses of EDP in education, and (3) student education about computers, to help meet the future demand for people familiar with EDP.

EDUCATIONAL INFORMATION SYSTEMS

New England Educational Data Systems (NEEDS) [10]

The NEEDS program began on a modest basis in 1960 as the Data Processing Project of the New England School Development Council, in cooperation with the Newton, Massachusetts, public schools, and supported by the School and University Program for Research and Development at Harvard University. The recipient of a large grant from the Ford Foundation, NEEDS expanded its program to provide a variety of computerized services for up to 100 school systems in 1966, as well as for 6 state departments of education and various cooperating universities in the New England region.

[10] G. Ernest Anderson, Jr., *Educational Data Processing Newsletter,* Vol. 3, No. 1 (January 1964), pp. 1–2.

In addition to performing routine activities pertaining to schedules, report cards, attendance, and testing, the NEEDS program is designed to train school personnel in educational applications of data processing technology. At the level of sophistication already achieved, a computer can assign 1,500 high school students to 200 courses in approximately 2 minutes. NEEDS scheduled approximately 20 secondary schools, ranging in size from 350 to 2,500 students, for the opening of classes in September 1964. In addition, member schools recently received 60,000 student report cards processed by the organization.

NEEDS is a model of regional cooperation in educational data processing, involving local school districts, state departments of education, and colleges and universities. The primary aim of the program is to improve operational procedures in education with an ultimate view to individualizing instruction. To realize this goal, NEEDS has identified the following program interests: (1) to eliminate information processing inefficiencies resulting from traditional procedures of record-keeping; (2) to provide rapid, reliable, and accurate information for the use of state and federal agencies in their planning and financing of education; (3) to establish effective machinery for relating research to the day-to-day life of the school system; (4) to bring technological improvements within the economic range of the public schools; (5) to develop personnel with technological skills in both education and data processing; and (6) to close the gap between the sophisticated level of data processing in business and the low level of data processing in schools.

Total Information Service (TIS) [11]

The Bureau of Data Processing of the Chicago Board of Education is presently operating what is believed to be the largest and most sophisticated EDP system in school districts, utilizing three IBM-1401 computers, one IBM-7074 computer, and a professional staff of eighty-three, which includes thirty-five systems analysts and computer programmers. The Data Processing Center of Chicago

[11] *AEDS Bulletin,* Association for Educational Data Systems, Vol. 1, No. 11 (October 1963), p. 1.

schools is employed in around-the-clock operations, with teaching and research applications scheduled during the day and administrative applications at night. This installation is considered to be a landmark, not only because of its anticipated efficient collection and economical conversion procedures, but also because of its attempt to develop a "total system approach" to data processing in schools.

An optical scanner, the first of its kind to be used in school applications, has recently been delivered to the Chicago center. This equipment will provide a means of reading class lists and other pupil records into the system. Unlike the optical scanners that recognize the presence or absence of marks in predetermined positions, this reader converts typewritten and other printed materials into coded input to the computer. Volume of input is expected to reach twenty-five million documents within five years.

The optical scanner is used, for example, in keeping records of student attendance. In this application, immediate plans call for the preparation once every five weeks of over 20,000 class rosters which would contain the names of over 600,000 children. These rosters, in multiple form, will be sent to the classrooms. A teacher's only responsibility will be to mark each student's absence or tardiness on the document. The names of students leaving the class will simply be crossed out with a pencil. The names of new students will be typed on the list by school clerks. When the rosters are returned to the computer center, they will be read by the optical scanner. It is expected that this record will eventually be produced every week.

All development is planned as a part of a total information system. The key is the development of an organization record for every facility, whether it be a school, a central office department, or a warehouse unit. The organization record is built up from factors such as the purpose of the room; the qualifications a teacher must have to teach the subject; the availability of additional support with respect to counselors, libraries, adjustment teachers, and so forth. In the organization record, the system goes so far as to identify the playground facilities that go with the school, the boilers and air conditioning units that serve it, and the visual aid

71

equipment available. As day-to-day transactions in finance, personnel turnover, materials, truck schedules, and student information are performed, data flow across the organization record so that it may be kept up to date.

The total system applications of the Chicago Bureau of Data Processing are grouped within six major categories: (1) budget and finance, (2) personnel and payroll, (3) materials, (4) student accounting and student scheduling, (5) instruction in the computer sciences, and (6) research.

Unlimited Personnel Data Through Automation Technology in Education (UPDATE) [12]

In 1962–63, the Iowa Center for Research in School Administration began an educational data processing project in cooperation with the College of Education of the State University of Iowa, the Measurement Research Center, the Iowa State Department of Public Instruction, and six pilot school districts. The objective was to introduce computer systems into Iowa schools in order to provide local districts with increased capacity to deal with intricate and massive data problems and to facilitate educational research through applications of data processing and computer science.

Assisted by a recent grant from the Ford Foundation to the State University, this educational data system will gather comprehensive, continuous information on school operations and pupil performance for the entire state of Iowa. This computer-based system will speed and expand the collection, processing, and analysis of data important to school administration and planning. It also will advance the study of environmental influences on student achievement. The center plans to collect information about all phases of educational programs in the state: students, teachers, supervisors, counselors, school boards, parents, school organization, curricula, administrative practices, programs of special services, and facilities. For instance, in order to gain better insight into student achievement, the center will gather and relate census data

[12] Personal correspondence from Alvin Grossman, Director of Research and Development for the Center in Educational Data Processing, California State Department of Education.

72

on teacher preparation, pupil-teacher ratios, and backgrounds of students and teachers.

Services to be developed using EDP include registering and scheduling classes, assigning lockers and auditorium seats, sectioning homerooms and classes by achievement, accounting for attendance, preparing honor lists, reporting pupil progress, preparing guidance reports, assigning teachers, maintaining activity fund records, providing inventories of library materials and audiovisual equipment, and preparing budgets, payrolls, requisitions, purchase orders, fiscal reports, and bus routes. In addition, UPDATE will provide services most Iowa school administrators do not now have, such as enrollment projections, building utilization analyses, financial projections, and unit cost analyses.

The Iowa Center program is highly significant in that it is designed to provide the entire range of educational data, from administrative and planning facts on the one hand to student achievement and environmental information on the other. If successful, the Iowa project should offer solutions to the problems of determining what data to gather, how to collect the necessary information, and how to use this information effectively. It should provide more data to support educational decision-making and should therefore increase both the speed and the accuracy of the process. Development of the data system will be carried out by the Iowa Educational Information Center in cooperation with the Iowa State Department of Public Instruction.

Cooperative Plan for Guidance and Admission (CPGA) [13]

CPGA, a project of the Educational Testing Service in Princeton, New Jersey, is an approach to the solution of a pressing educational problem—that of organizing, summarizing, and communicating all the important information that high schools collect about students. CPGA was developed initially in Georgia, with support from the Ford Foundation and the Educational Testing Service. CPGA involves cooperative action by educators and employers of a state or region toward the following goals: (1) development of a "common language" and a "universal code" to be used by all schools and colleges in the recording and transmitting of information about students, (2) application of modern electronic techniques (high-speed computers) for summarizing and communicating information about students, (3) evolution of a system to feed back information to the high schools so that they know the degree of success achieved by their graduates in jobs and colleges or universities, and (4) reduction of costs of student record-keeping while improving efficiency.

The CPGA plan uses a standardized set of materials to record the entire record of a student, including both curricular and extracurricular activities. At the end of the eleventh grade, all this information is manually transcribed onto documents readable by a machine or is transmitted via punched cards. During the summer, these data are processed, printed, and returned to the school on a multiple-part form.

This report presents a detailed picture of each student's progress in a standard format. When a student requests a transcript during his senior year, one copy of the form is updated and mailed. This form also provides space for a college or university to return information to the high school, thus enabling schools to evaluate their educational programs.

At its computer facility in Princeton, the Educational Testing Service is coordinating the processing of materials and now releases computer programs and procedures to state education departments and universities desiring local use of CPGA.

California Pilot Project in Educational Data Processing [14]

The roots of the California Pilot Project in Educational Data Processing lie in the 1959–60 work of the State Advisory Committee on Integrated Data Processing, a group appointed by the State Superintendent of Public Instruction. This group examined the actual and potential uses of data processing for educational purposes. The results of the Committee's report led to the development of the State Pilot Project as an essential part of a master

[14] *A Report of an Experiment—The State Pilot Project in Educational Data Processing* (Richmond, Calif.: Richmond City Schools, July 1964).

74

plan for integrated data processing in California schools. The pilot project, completed in 1963, represents the trial phase of the broad program. The second phase is now underway in Sacramento at the Research and Development Center in Educational Data Processing of the State Department of Education. The third and final phase will be the actual establishment of regional data processing centers to serve California school districts.

The California Pilot Project is significant because it demonstrates that a regional cooperative venture in educational data processing is feasible. After three years of experimentation, the state project concluded that large districts, those with an average of twenty thousand or more students in daily attendance, and organized regional groupings, embracing several districts within each region, could operate data processing systems with foreseeably good results. It also concluded that the regional type of system offers economic and qualitative advantages over local systems regardless of size.

The first California regional data processing center began its operations in Sacramento in July 1965. Here, at the first of twelve centers planned to serve hundreds of schools throughout the state, forty-four school districts in sixteen counties are scheduling student programs, printing attendance reports, and storing students' grades and test scores.

The general purpose of the Research and Development Center in Educational Data Processing is to provide, through research and through the development of model systems and techniques, a basis of knowledge and methodology that can be used to advantage in the establishment of regional data processing centers throughout the state and in the upgrading of district systems already in operation. The specific purposes are: (1) to design and develop model systems for collecting and handling data to meet the requirements of pupil personnel and curricular functions, including the analysis of existing systems and a planned transition to more effective systems; (2) to conduct research and development in facilitating computer applications by means of programming aids such as compilers and report generators; (3) to conduct simulation studies in such areas as data processing (pretrial of new systems) and in specific applications, such as scheduling, guidance, validation of counseling procedures, and curriculum changes; (4) to establish and maintain a library and clearing house for information relevant to educational data processing methods, systems, and equipment; (5) to develop proposals for cooperative establishment of compatible systems for the mutual benefit of local school systems; and (6) to evaluate and analyze available data processing equipment and develop specifications for new equipment and its educational use.

RESEARCH

Computer-assisted Scheduling [15]

Thousands of schools face the onerous task of assigning pupils to sections according to a master schedule. Practical procedures now exist that mechanize all or substantial parts of these procedures, permitting the completion in minutes or hours of tasks that formerly required weeks or months of professional time.

Initial experiments were applied to college scheduling. One of the earliest was Blakesley's at Purdue University, beginning in 1956, which aimed at devising a computer system for registering, scheduling, and assessing fees for all students in order to improve a student's choice of courses and the overall utilization of resources. Other colleges and universities, including the University of Massachusetts, the University of Rhode Island, and MIT, developed similar computer programs. IBM worked out a 7090 computer program based on an early Purdue model. Subsequently, Notre Dame, the University of Illinois, and other institutions of higher education experimented with programs written for the IBM-709 or 7090 computers that could section students for the larger universities. Holz developed such a program for MIT. Blakesley has since then refined his Purdue program to schedule over eighteen thousand students in less than six hours of computer time and produce an assortment of class lists, enrollment reports,

[15] *Journal of Educational Data Processing,* Research and Development Center in Educational Data Processing, Educational Systems Corporation, Sacramento, Calif., Vol. 1, No. 2 (May 1964). The entire issue is devoted to description of computer-assisted scheduling programs.

and other by-products. The next step in the Purdue project, now in the experimental stage, will be the computerized construction of an "optimum" schedule of classes.

Other research in scheduling is presently being devoted to the complex task of automating the master schedule in secondary school educational programs. Much of this work, such as the studies directed by Holzman at the University of Pittsburgh, is concentrated on building a theoretical model. Research is based on the use of computers in the anticipated flexible schools of the future in which each student is expected to proceed at his own pace, without grade limitations, and with an individual and constantly changing schedule. Comprehensive investigations of the methods of developing these complex scheduling programs are currently underway at various centers, including SDC in Santa Monica, California; the California State Department of Education's Center for Research and Development in Educational Data Processing in Sacramento, California; and Generalized Academic Simulation Programs (GASP) at MIT. The GASP programs, theoretical in character, offer considerable promise for assigning time, classrooms, instructors, and students to the classes required by a school's curriculum and a student's needs.

The IBM CLASS (Class Load and Student Scheduling) [16] and the California Richmond Union High School computer program named SOCRATES (Scheduling of Classes Realized Automatically Through Effortless Systemization) are additional research efforts in the direction of more effective scheduling in secondary schools. Anderson has developed a program somewhat similar to IBM's CLASS which has been coded for the IBM-7090 computer and is used by a number of school systems in the New England School Development Council (NESDEC).

One practical outcome of theoretical investigations of this kind is a scheduling program devised by Oakford and others at Stanford University's School of Education, under a grant from the Fund for the Advancement of Education. Bush and Allen introduced the Stanford programs into five West Coast school systems during

[16] Not to be confused with the System Development Corporation's Computer-based Laboratory for Automated School Systems, also called CLASS.

77

the school year 1963–64. Three schools in California, one in Oregon, and one in Nevada were scheduled in whole or in part by the Stanford programs, and more than twenty-five schools in the region were in various stages of planning this scheduling for 1964–65. One high school in San Jose, California, used the system only for student assignment. In Stockton, California, however, Lincoln High School developed a master schedule for an experimental program. Homestead High School in Sunnyvale, California, used the Stanford programs to construct the schedule for an educational design that is gradually incorporating many innovations, including team teaching.

The Stanford scheduling system's biggest undertaking to date has been the scheduling of Marshall High School, in Portland, Oregon, which enrolls approximately two thousand students in a highly experimental program. Marshall High School is characterized by twenty-one daily time modules of twenty minutes each which can be scheduled singly or in combination, school-wide team teaching, independent study averaging one third of each student's time, the organization of instruction into small, medium-size, or large groups, and many other interesting innovations.

Computer-based Laboratory
for Automated School Systems (CLASS) [17]

SDC has been using a very sophisticated computer facility, designated CLASS, for the research and development of an instructional system designed to provide optimal learning conditions. CLASS permits simultaneous automated instruction of twenty students; each student receives an individualized sequence of instructional materials adapted to his particular needs, or he learns in a group mediated by the teacher or computer. Application of modern data processing technology to other functions normally associated with a school district also can be employed in CLASS.

In the CLASS system, each student has a manually operated film viewer containing two thousand frames of instructional ma-

[17] John F. Cogswell and Don D. Bushnell, "A Computer-based Laboratory for Automation in School Systems," *Audio Visual Communication Review* (July–August 1961), pp. 173–85.

terial. In addition, he has a response device, linked to the computer, which indicates the sequence of slides to be seen by the student, enables the student to respond to questions, and presents knowledge of results to the student in the form of a coded light. The computer maintains performance records for all students, supplying these records to the teacher, counselor, or administrator.

Provision is made for two teachers in CLASS. Each teacher has console facilities that make it possible for him to call up computer-generated displays showing the current progress of any student or group of students. Automatic alarm lights alert the teacher to students who are performing unsuccessfully in any lesson. CLASS also permits instruction through media such as television, films and slides, and conventional lecture and textbook methods, permitting individual or group instruction. Studies of the impact of automation on the roles of guidance, instructional, and administrative personnel can readily be carried out.

Programmed Logic for Automatic
Teaching Operation (PLATO) [18]

Another computer research facility in automated teaching is PLATO, a project being developed in the Coordinated Science Laboratory of the University of Illinois. The main objective of PLATO is to provide a system capable of tutoring a large number of students concurrently in a variety of subject materials.

To accomplish this aim, the system uses a high-speed digital computer as the executive control element. As the students' requests arrive at the computer, they are accepted and processed sequentially. Computer speed permits all student requests to be processed without noticeable delay. Besides acting as the control element, the computer records the students' requests and later processes the records for information about both students and lesson material. Changes are usually implemented by altering the computer program instead of by rewiring student stations.

Because of the flexibility of the PLATO system, improvement in automatic instruction is viewed as a two-dimensional process:

[18] Donald L. Bitzer, "PLATO: An Automatic Teaching Device," *IRE Transactions on Education* (December 1961).

first, there is improvement in the content and organization of lesson material. Second, there is improvement in pedagogy, especially strategies of teaching. An attempt is being made to develop a system that will adapt itself to each student's immediate needs by measuring the student's performance and determining his difficulties and characteristic behavior. With this knowledge, alternate approaches are provided for the student when one approach has not met with sufficient success. The ultimate purpose is a cumulative record of student behavior in an effort to refine the most appropriate teaching strategy for him.

Computer Simulation

With the advent of the digital computer, simulation techniques have been used productively for purposes in addition to instruction, such as analyzing an operational man-machine system and aiding in the development of an advanced system design. The complexity and detail with which the system can be simulated and the variety of techniques used to study, manipulate, and alter the system in order to achieve new objectives or to monitor ongoing functions were not possible before computers came into use. For analytical purposes, simulation has all the traditional advantages of the laboratory over contextual or field research. Whenever a real system is too large for observation, laboratory simulation can be used.

At Purdue University and in the St. Louis junior college district, for example, simulation techniques are being used to forecast building and staff requirements under varying academic conditions. At SDC, under a U.S. Office of Education grant, computer simulation has been utilized to study various types of secondary school organization as they affect the implementation of innovations in school practice—particularly space utilization, school organization, the handling of information, and the role and duties of teachers. Experimenters have simulated one thousand students going through a nongraded school, with a view to comparing the number of steps required by both "slow" and "fast" students in completing a given unit of work. Important insight into individualized instruction is thus obtained. The goal of the project is to use the simulation model to study changes in school structure and operation, with a documentation of the time utilized in each activity.

COMPUTER EDUCATION [19]

Knowledge of EDP techniques is recognized as a valuable complement to progressive high school and junior college education. No student ought to leave school without some understanding of automation and information processing, considering the important changes these are bringing to the adult world.

Most of the existing formal preparation in EDP has come from colleges and universities. Because of the current and predicted future demand for trained students in EDP, in engineering, in business machine operations, and in related fields, colleges and universities have stepped up their curricula in these areas and expanded their computing facilities. The trend in many institutions has been toward open shop computing centers available to both faculty and students in any discipline. With the teletypewriting stations linked to the computing center, classrooms and laboratories become substations for program checkout and problem solving. Excellent examples of both the open computing center and teletypewriter stations may be found at MIT, Stanford University, and the University of Oklahoma. Forty-five colleges and universities with data processing courses for both secondary school teachers and students are listed in the *Project on Information Processing Newsletter*.[20] Unfortunately, only a few courses offer instruction related specifically to educational data processing.

Since its acceptance in the colleges and universities, data processing instruction has been introduced into technical and vocational high school, post–high school, and adult training programs. The President's Panel on Scientific and Technical Manpower reported that sixty-nine thousand data processing technicians will be needed annually over the next decade, yet only about twenty-five thousand are entering the labor force each year. A bulletin available from

[19] Fred Gruenberger, "Computer Training and Education," *Datamation* (May 1963).
[20] See Appendix C.

the U.S. Government Printing Office entitled *Employment Outlook for Electronic Computer Operating Personnel and for Programmers* and a pamphlet released by the National Science Teachers Association called *Careers in Electronic Data Processing* [21] are both valuable references for counseling and guidance personnel and sources of factual material. A central problem here, of course, is the rapid outdating of competencies required in the field.

Through support from Title VIII of the National Defense Education Act, many states have developed educational programs for training individuals to become skilled EDP technicians. Typical course offerings include training in keypunch operations, wiring of unit record equipment, computer programming, and systems analysis. Examples of vocational training programs that include extensive courses in data processing are those offered in the ten centers and schools throughout the state of Washington, in the Iowa Technical Education Center in Ottumwa, and in the long-established program at the Dobbins Technical High School in Philadelphia. A directory of *Schools Conducting Title VIII Preparatory or Extension Data Processing Technology Courses* [22] may be obtained from the Director of the Technical Education Branch of the U.S. Office of Education. Also available from the same office is a Technical Education Series curriculum outline for a two-year course in post–high school instruction in programming and business applications.

Computer training in higher education, however, does not reach enough students. Roughly one out of every three high school students does not graduate; a second does not continue his education beyond a high school diploma; and so only the third, the college-bound student, will benefit from EDP courses offered in higher education. To fill this gap and to prepare other students for technical training or college courses in which the computer is used, secondary school administrators and teachers have begun to follow the lead of technical schools and universities. For example, the computer instructional program for the Chicago public schools includes a two-year course of study at the junior college level

[21] See Appendix C for both titles.
[22] See Appendix C.

82

for the training of programmers and four semesters of preparation for prospective teachers of data processing. In addition, a pilot program for high school seniors is being planned in two Chicago schools this year. It is anticipated that this offering will be extended to all fifty-five Chicago high schools within a two-year period.

Some other school districts are justifying the purchase or rental of a small or medium-sized computer system by using it primarily in the teaching of mathematics, programming, computer system operation and maintenance, and related subjects. Since the advent of problem-oriented computer languages, even young students can acquire the programming skills necessary for using the computer in a variety of subject areas. The use of mathematical models, heretofore unavailable to the secondary student, has now become possible for schools with access to computing facilities. By using the computer, students gain a better understanding of problem analysis and acquire computing skills through first-hand experience with the machines. In a report entitled *Computer Oriented Mathematics,* issued after a conference sponsored by the National Council of Teachers of Mathematics in 1963, more than fifty schools were mentioned as having concentrated courses ranging from traditional applications (for example, trigonometry and simultaneous equations) to mathematical research and advanced puzzle problems.

To encourage this trend, the Project on Information Processing of the National Teachers Association at Montclair State College in New Jersey has made available kits of materials for ninth-grade general science classes that include theory, operations, and uses of electronic computers. An introduction to instruction in computer-oriented mathematics for secondary school teachers is available from the National Council of Teachers of Mathematics. Course materials and assistance in establishing instructional programs in local schools are available from local chapters of the Association for Computing Machinery and from the Data Processing Management Association, which has a special program for "Future Data Processors."

The fact that there has been a scarcity of secondary school teachers who are prepared to teach computer mathematics courses has been a major problem. Some progress is being made, however.

The National Science Foundation and Title VIII of the NDEA sponsor summer institute programs for teachers. The passage of the Elementary and Secondary Education Act of 1965 has also opened up new opportunities for developing EDP curriculum programs in teacher education institutions.

In summarizing the rapid development of computer instruction in secondary schools, Harry L. Phillips of the U.S. Office of Education delivered a paper at the 1964 Annual Convention of the American Association of School Administrators in which he said:

> The computer as an instructional device in science and mathematics programs in secondary schools has had a colorful and rapidly developing history. This has ranged from a very sophisticated rigorous mathematical approach such as is employed by Dr. Irving Dodes at the Bronx High School of Science where the students have ready access to a very elaborate computing facility to a program in which Professor Richard V. Andree, at the University of Oklahoma, has transported students as far as 300 miles to involve them in a Saturday computer education course in Norman, Oklahoma. (Significant computer-oriented instructional programs are being developed in the Greater Philadelphia area, Chicago, Detroit, Des Moines, Washington, D.C., Boston, Buffalo, Seattle, Palo Alto, Minneapolis–St. Paul, Pittsburgh, Miami, Norman, New York City, and many other localities.)

Conclusion

Automated methods have found limited but rapidly growing application and acceptance when there are masses of fairly precise data related to well-defined tasks, when processing is highly repetitive, when the rules for decisions can be specified with great precision, when it is necessary or desirable to repeat processes many times under varying conditions, when data are to be analyzed by "brute force" heuristic methods rather than according to a logical plan, and when there is great demand for high speed or multiple precision. When the computer has been applied appropriately to educational data, it has reduced the amount of professional time and energy previously devoted to clerical work; it has reduced the unit cost of processing educational data; and it has facilitated the development of new techniques, resources, insights, and processes not feasible under manual or tabulating machine systems.

Perhaps one of the most valuable results of the introduction of EDP technology into education has been the accompanying need to examine with precision the nature of educational rules, procedures, schedules, objectives, and assumptions. If automated processes must provide for a variety of future events and contingencies, these must be anticipated and defined without ambiguity. Since machines will in general do only what their operators cause them to do (assuming no random malfunctioning), those who design EDP systems must understand both the characteristics of the machines—and hence the state-of-the-art as a whole—and the requirements that the machines are to satisfy.

One aspect of the present state-of-the-art is certainly the state of mind of the educator as he considers the present and possible uses and effects of EDP. When educators place increased reliance on mechanical processes, they must understand what these processes imply. Mere access to more data does not ensure wise selection or use of such data. It is fair to say that the general technology has advanced well beyond our application of it. The most striking feature of the state-of-the-art is the disparity between practice and potential, both in the nature and scope of applications and in the breadth of understanding and acceptance of the power of these applications to improve education.

4

Advancing
the
Field

In the process of reviewing recent developments in the use of electronic data processing in education, as compared with computer use in other fields, we became increasingly aware of certain pressing problems and issues.

In checking the validity of our tentative conclusions regarding these problems and issues, we were fortunate in having a significant data source, in addition to our review of current practice, to draw upon. Funds made available through the Cooperative Research Program of the U.S. Office of Education provided the resources not only for collecting data but also for assembling a discussion group charged with the following responsibilities: (1) to identify problems and issues pertaining to automated school information systems, (2) to suggest needed research and development, and (3) to set forth criteria designed to assist funding agencies in judging the merits of research and development proposals submitted to them.

This conference, held at Lake Arrowhead, California, opened windows on the thoughts and activities of persons actively engaged in or concerned about EDP in education. The thirty-seven conferees [1] included specialists in educational data processing, teachers, curriculum and guidance specialists, administrators, psychologists, information scientists, and research workers. They represented state departments of education, public and private schools, colleges and universities, and various associations. Most of those in attendance prepared brief papers in advance, summarizing what they considered to be problems and gaps in school information systems as well as areas in need of research and development.

In essence, the character of the Lake Arrowhead Conference might be summarized in one word: "disagreement." Clearly, both the primary concerns and the vocabulary of specialists in EDP and of practicing educators frequently differ markedly. Furthermore, disagreements regarding priorities and relevant issues occur within each group.

In spite of frustrations and difficulties, however, certain agreements were implicit among the conference participants: the need for uniform definitions and terminology, the need for educators and technologists to work together more closely in automating school information systems, and the prevalent fear of the machine among educators. Some of the most significant disagreements focused on the following: what the computer can and cannot do, the role of computers in assisting teachers in their instructional acts, the use of time saved by automating educational processes, the preparation of material for computer processing, the uses of processed data, the special training of EDP personnel in education, and the educational lag in employing the new technology. Only the most superficial of discussions could produce quick agreement on topics so fraught with issues!

In the development of automated educational information systems, EDP specialists and school practitioners such as teachers, curriculum directors, guidance specialists, and administrators must be brought together frequently and for many purposes. In the planning and conduct of these necessary confrontations, the problem of communication cannot be over-estimated.

This chapter begins by presenting the criteria suggested by the

[1] See Appendix A for their names and affiliations.

Lake Arrowhead Conference for funding research and development projects. The conferees did such a thorough job on this aspect that their list of suggestions is presented here almost as it appeared initially. The next section, drawing on tape recordings from the Conference and data presented in earlier chapters, discusses the significant problems and issues to be resolved in order to advance the use of automated methods in educational information systems and presents recommendations for solving these problems.

Criteria for Funding Projects

The coming years will undoubtedly produce thousands of requests to governmental and philanthropic agencies for the financial support of projects designed to advance the understanding and use of computers and other electronic devices in educational information systems. The questions formulated below provide essentially nonsubstantive or process criteria that might be applied in the consideration of these proposals. Recommendations set forth in the subsequent section suggest some of the substantive concerns to which these criteria might be applied.

1. Will the results of the project be generalizable; that is, will they benefit agencies or groups other than the one being developed or investigated? For example, cost is a significant and often prohibitive factor for school districts. It would be immeasurably helpful if more data were available pertaining to costs of various kinds of systems in varying sizes and combinations of school districts.

2. Are there provisions in the proposal to facilitate dissemination and replication? Often the preparation of a project report satisfies the information needs of only a small audience. Replication is impossible unless full details regarding purposes, procedures, and findings are provided.

3. Will the project advance educational goals by removing a roadblock or otherwise resolving a recognized problem? For example, computerized methods of scheduling facilitate the develop-

ment of highly individualized student programs in secondary schools. Similarly, the computer may very well play a key role in guiding pupil placements in elementary schools, employing many items of personal data in arriving at each decision.

4. Is the proposed project both cumulative, in that it builds on what is already known, and innovative, in that it proposes to create new tools, techniques, or knowledge? The project proposal should reveal the investigator's knowledge of the field and indicate rather precisely how he intends to add to what is known.

5. Will the project provide for more efficient use of existing knowledge, techniques, and tools? For example, the tedious counseling process of predicting student success on the basis of past performances is vastly expedited through the use of EDP equipment.

6. Does the project offer promise of maximizing scarce resources of time, money, and personnel? For example, assistant superintendents for teacher personnel and for instruction often become so bogged down with detail that their proper jobs—for which nobody else is as well prepared—go begging. Many of their routine information processing chores might well be automated.

7. Does the project offer promise of improving research conditions or school practices in some significant educational realm? For example, highly sensitive pupil placement and instructional procedures based on many factors of child development and subsequent research into the consequences of these educational decisions simply could not be contemplated without access to the computer.

8. If the project is to have significance for a wide range of school systems and personnel, have the capabilities of intended users been accounted for? Use of the results may require a sophistication not generally available in the intended application settings, or it may be necessary to mount subsequent in-service training programs.

9. If the project can be consequential only if activities continue beyond termination of the grant, are funds available for self-sustainment? Or will there be a need for continual infusion of

outside funds? The hope is that educational institutions will eventually become financially self-sufficient in EDP if outside agencies provide research and development funds to meet the initial and most burdensome costs for the institutions.

10. Does the project offer promise of expanding the capabilities and applications of the EDP installation as the institution continues its utilization?

Obviously, not all these criteria are pertinent to every request for funds. Many are nothing more than criteria for judging any piece of research. But anyone experienced in reviewing grant requests knows how frequently such common-sense conditions are ignored or not understood by would-be investigators.

Since communication among the educational groups potentially involved in and affected by EDP in education is still far from adequate, funding agencies reviewing proposals for supporting grants should seek the advice of persons competent in *both* EDP and education. For some time to come, too, they must give high priority to effecting intersystem compatability and to maintaining good communication among educational systems and agencies through the development of common terminology, nomenclature, definitions, and standards. Funding agencies must also satisfy themselves that projects of an applied nature stand the test of use in actual settings.

Funding agencies can perform a most significant service simply by helping to implement in the context of education what is already known about EDP. Educational practice in this respect lags dangerously. The primary barriers appear to be the lack of knowledgeable personnel sufficiently high in the administrative structure to affect decision-making (most of today's educational leaders were born and formally educated in a precomputer era); the inadequacy of resources for getting started, especially for moving from simple punched card methods to the use of a computer; and general ignorance and indifference within the education profession regarding automated information processing. The story of human evolution testifies to the ignorance, indifference, and superstition that man has overcome. But the continued presence of these shortcomings within the ranks of those charged with dispelling such frailties always comes as a sobering, if not chilling, realization.

Problems, Issues, and Recommendations

In seeking to classify what is needed for the advancement of any aspect of education, one is tempted to separate research from description and analysis and to separate both of these from a variety of applied and developmental activities. We have resisted this temptation here because the recency of extensive use of EDP in education, the rapid increase in activity and interest, and the expansive speculation regarding the future all suggest an urgent need to keep research and development intimately allied. Instead, we have employed a set of rather functional categories (suggested by the Lake Arrowhead Conference and by analysis of the state-of-the-art) that facilitate discussion of problems and issues and presentation of recommendations cutting across the research-description-application spectrum. The categories are as follows: (1) electronic data systems, (2) EDP and innovations in the school program, (3) education for using EDP, (4) the collection and dissemination of EDP lore, and (5) other unsolved problems. Naturally, there is considerable overlap of specific problems within these general areas; nonetheless, this clustering is useful. The recommendations are relevant to many groups but are frequently phrased as though directed primarily to funding agencies.

ELECTRONIC DATA SYSTEMS

The field of education suffers significantly from both fear of computer omnipotence and lack of imagination regarding computer utility. The analogy of the human brain in explaining computer capabilities has been overdrawn. The computer can do only what some human has programmed it to do—admittedly with superlative efficiency. On the other hand, educators are slow to comprehend the myriad tasks that computers are equipped to do and that might be readily programmed for them. For the cure of these twin ills, *we recommend the development of an en-*

92

lightened, continuing program of information for educators regarding the technology of automated educational data processing systems. The modern educator need not necessarily understand the inner workings of a computer, but he must have a grasp of what this machine, linked to other electronic devices, can do.

Some confusion prevails regarding the appropriateness for education of equipment designed primarily for business, industrial, and military needs. Actually, the needs of education do not exceed the general-purpose nature of computer hardware. Computer software, however, must be designed specifically for education. Costs of hardware and software may very well necessitate some unique cooperative strategies among schools and school systems in getting full return on their investments. But the availability of computers engineered specifically for education is not the problem. The educator's unique problems are in programming, but even here many general techniques are applicable. To counteract prevailing misconceptions, *it is recommended that studies be conducted to determine the special hardware and software requirements of EDP in education.*

The problem of where to place the automated data processing system in the structure of school district organization in order to get maximal usage is still relatively unexplored. *We recommend, therefore, that studies be designed and supported to determine how the user can get full value from the system and how systems can be designed to assure responsiveness to a wide range of demands.* Management studies similar to the one conducted by the McKinsey Corporation would be appropriate. The McKinsey study focused on discerning what factors contributed to more profitable use of EDP by major industrial users. The study revealed that the most successful users had the approval of a top management familiar with the potentialities of EDP. Thus, the data processing design team was located at a management level high enough to allow it to take a broad look at the problems. The systems that developed under these circumstances more than paid for the costs.

Some of the most complex problems in designing data systems for education arise from the difficulty of determining the minimal basic items required for information processing tasks, especially in these times of educational change. Until some of these guidelines are available, school districts will be reluctant to enter into cooperative data processing ventures on state or regional bases for fear that the information to be processed will not adequately serve their needs. And yet, for economy and efficiency, collaboration among school districts, particularly small ones, appears to be highly desirable and, in some instances, necessary. Recognition should be given to recent software developments that allow some flexibility in the creation of systems under circumstances where it is difficult to specify the exact initial data requirements. *We recommend that studies be supported that propose to set forth basic minimal data items for information processing in various aspects of education (facilities, teacher personnel, budget, students, curriculum, and so on) at several different levels (i.e., for local single districts, local combinations of districts, states, regions, and the nation).* Projects might well develop handbooks as aids to standardizing terminology and definitions.

Studies of this kind provide only part of the information needed to design systems that satisfy the inter-dependent demands of schools and agencies. The ultimate need for compatibility among data processing systems should be recognized and planned for at the outset of involvement with EDP.

Problems pertaining to the compatibility of separate data processing systems emerge again and again: What are the potentialities of state, regional, and even national programs? Can the needs of local school systems be met adequately by a remote storage and retrieval unit? What kinds of data can be gathered to serve the interests of the many cooperating school systems appropriately? At present, school systems are not alike in their designations of responsibility for decision-making or in the identification of essential data. Consequently, one technologist's "total system" becomes another's subsystem. Different groups of people require different sets of data, and there is little agreement on the terminology for describing individual needs. This quagmire of problems occurs in every major field of application of EDP. The practical limitations that cut a system down to size are the dollars, time, and intellectual resources available to the design team as well as the political interactions among the potential users. *It is recommended that studies investigate procedures for establishing and maintaining compatibility among EDP systems of varying sizes and complexity.*

Studies of minimal data item requirements and of compatibility among EDP systems would lay the groundwork for studies designed to determine the kinds of software necessary to broad-scale operation of EDP in education. Much of what is needed is standard for users in other fields, but the commercial production of what is not standard may very well be held up until assurance of marketability is forthcoming.

The interrelated nature of the studies recommended in this section on electronic data systems places special responsibility on investigators and funding agency personnel alike. With very little revision or additional work, a project proposal in one of these areas might be amended to cover additional areas. When separate but potentially supporting studies are funded simultaneously, agency officials could be of service in bringing investigators into communication with each other. Such communication might very well lead to systematic assessment of the special needs of education likely to be encountered when the use of EDP becomes firmly established.

ELECTRONIC DATA PROCESSING AND INNOVATIONS IN THE SCHOOL PROGRAM

Automated scheduling of the course loads of students in secondary schools has already been successfully demonstrated. The need now is for large numbers of high schools to take this significant step. Furthermore, most demonstrations have involved schools using relatively traditional patterns of organization and group instruction. The use of EDP in scheduling highly individualized programs for schools seeking to modify conventional procedures is only beginning to open up.

The kinds of decisions educators make determine the kinds of data they need for making them wisely. Conversely, the kinds of data available frequently predetermine the kinds of decisions

95

with which educators concern themselves. In the immediate past (and predominantly at present) educators buttressed their estimates of student ability and progress with standardized intelligence and achievement test results, when such information was available. And these were essentially the only diagnostic data available to them. Furthermore, these data fitted the prevailing concept of what education was for, and vice versa.

As we move today toward individualized programs facilitated by new patterns of school organization and comprehensive packages of instructional materials, the pupil diagnoses and prescriptions called for demand new data and more sophisticated use of them. Most teachers have not yet either perceived or been prepared for the kinds of decisions that they will increasingly be called upon to make. Furthermore, they usually do not yet see the inherent possibilities of the many items of information now available. It is imperative, therefore, that educators stay very close to the tasks of defining, collecting, and providing the data needed. Otherwise, EDP personnel are likely to develop systems that perpetuate the provision of data pertinent to the relatively routine educational tasks of the past but inappropriate to the sensitive educational decisions of the future. A new kind of school is emerging, calling for new kinds of data about students and their learning and, therefore, for the closest collaboration of educator and information specialist in collecting these data. To advance this collaboration, *we recommend that support be given to projects seeking to couple automated data processing techniques with the development of innovations in scheduling, counseling, school organization, curriculum development, and instruction.* Such projects may well reveal how "the new school" might look if a whole range of educational changes were to be introduced simultaneously.

If, for example, individualized instruction is to become more than a slogan, conceptualization and electronic processing of data are essential for guiding diagnosis and providing the information on consequences of decisions that will facilitate reassessment of students and methods. This is a tall and expensive order, since it centers on the use of EDP for opening up fresh possibilities in what is now a primitive part of the educational enterprise. The quantities and varieties of data to be stored and retrieved to carry out this innovation, to say nothing of the data manipulations required, defy human capabilities. This function of EDP would thus entail little automation of what is already manually operative. We are now beginning to envision for the teacher a highly professional role of diagnosing and prescribing for the learner. But this role may never be fulfilled unless the computer is brought meaningfully and productively into these sensitive, often intuitive acts, as supplier of essential data and as predictor of certain possible consequences of choice. As yet this fertile soil has scarcely been turned over.

Many of the projects seeking to carry out this recommendation are likely to be related in some way to the forward thrust of American education generally. For example, when the traditional ways of placing children in grades and classes are stripped away through the creation of nongraded, team-taught schools, what kinds of data will be needed by teachers seeking to take advantage of their new organizational flexibility? Can such data be programmed efficiently for computer processing and then be retrieved to be employed effectively in teachers' decision-making? Can this be done economically? Similar kinds of questions about determining appropriate curricular sequences might well be investigated. Unique possibilities for monitoring or for simulating learning and teaching strategies are also opened up. The search for learning environments responsive to individual needs also suggests much more extensive and sensitive use of the computer in storing and retrieving instructional materials.

The projects suggested here extend far beyond the automation of school accounting, scheduling students, and scoring tests— activities that too often come rather exclusively to mind when the uses of computers in education are discussed. Furthermore, they suggest hitherto little explored roles for guidance counselors, especially in elementary schools where the functions of such personnel have never been clearly defined.

Extensive research in computer-based instruction, now beginning at Stanford University, the University of Illinois, the University of Pittsburgh, and a scattering of other centers, promises to provide significant insight into curricular sequences and learning strategies. Intercenter communication systems will provide quick exchange of information, facilitate replication of studies with different population samples, and permit students in one center to plug into experimental programs at another center many miles away. These investigations are likely to be expensive from the viewpoint of the volume of data handled in relation to the cost of the computers and other equipment required. But there is no way of putting a price tag on the worth of such activity in relation to the potential gains in understanding curricular and learning processes. *We recommend that such research programs move forward apace through substantial funding provisions.*

The broken-front character of educational change complicates the problem of interschool or interdistrict cooperation in developing experimental information processing systems because seldom are several schools simultaneously engaged in developing new innovations. Consequently, considerations other than volume of data in relation to cost must enter heavily into determining the merit of proposals. Funding agency personnel must be acutely attuned to the advancing front of school experimentation or draw heavily upon the advice of people who are.

EDUCATION FOR USING ELECTRONIC
DATA PROCESSING

The lag in using EDP in education is formidable. Simply to implement for education what is now commonplace in enlightened segments of other fields would produce startling changes in the educational fabric. The shortage of persons knowledgeable about both education and EDP is often blamed for much of the problem. The interface problem of translating educational processes into terms that can be manipulated by the computer is a formidable one. Educators do not know how to get data ready for the computer and are unable to use them when they come from the computer. Electronic data technologists ask for data in terms that are unfamiliar to and awkward for the educator to handle, and the data come back from the computer in equally puzzling forms.

98

For that matter, educators are unable to express their problems in language that can be easily interpreted by EDP specialists. Likewise, the problems that frequently fascinate the latter appear to many educators to be of secondary significance. For these reasons, successful information systems can be developed only if these two groups work closely together.

It is therefore simply impossible to overstate the need for educators and data processing personnel to come together in circumstances designed to promote mutual understanding and uncluttered avenues of communication. It is gratifying to note, therefore, an increasing number of short conferences in which leadership personnel representing many aspects of education are brought together to exchange information and seek answers to problems of EDP utilization. *We recommend increased activity of this kind, with participation offered to all educational personnel.*

A second problem is that educators themselves are far from agreed on the way to select and train persons knowledgeable about both education and EDP. The ultimate production of a steady stream of college graduates, some of whom will follow careers in education and whose curricula have included studies in computer science, offers a solution—but much too belatedly. Provision of courses directed to the educational applications of EDP in the pre-service and in-service programs of teachers offers an immediate but superficial solution. The problem is clear but the obvious solutions fail to promise relief that is both early and substantial. *We recommend, therefore, that projects be designed (1) to identify the formal education and direct experience that would be most helpful in enabling educators and EDP personnel to develop operational understanding of their respective domains, (2) to translate these training needs into sound instructional programs, and (3) to demonstrate these curricula and disseminate information about their effectiveness.*

THE COLLECTION AND DISSEMINATION OF ELECTRONIC DATA PROCESSING LORE

Although EDP is now used for a variety of purposes in American education, a body of lore based on actual experience is virtually nonexistent. As a result, there is much duplication of effort, repetition of mistakes, and waste of scarce human and material resources. The persons involved no doubt have been too busy actually applying EDP to keep detailed records of their successes and failures. What have been the experiences to date among those educational agencies already using automated information systems? What purposes did they set out to fulfill? What difficulties did they encounter and what solutions did they formulate? Even prolonged discussions among users produce only disjointed, noncumulative snapshots.

The successes, failures, and tribulations of the business and scientific communities in using automated information systems have been relatively well documented. Education must now develop its own body of lore about the problems and processes involved. Much useful experience already has been acquired by workers in the new vineyards. It simply needs to be collected, processed, bottled, and labeled for easy identification and use.

We recommend first, therefore, that studies be projected to identify problems and procedures in the development, utilization, supervision, and administration of automated school information systems. Specifically, some studies should focus on changes resulting from the implementation of EDP: in administrative and organizational structure, in personnel utilization, and in curriculum and instruction. Others should seek to develop taxonomies of the kinds of problems confronted and the relative usefulness of various approaches to their solution. Computer use is expensive. Until information of the kind suggested here is made readily available, these costs will be unnecessarily increased through duplication of questionable procedures.

Second, *we recommend that a national central clearing house be established, not as a repository of materials and programs but as a switching center for promoting the exchange of technical information and materials on EDP in education.* Its main function would be to provide information about who is doing what where, thus facilitating the exchange of views and activities among school districts, government agencies, and various other organiza-

100

tions or associations. The National Education Association or the U.S. Office of Education might appropriately perform such a function.

OTHER UNSOLVED PROBLEMS

Several additional kinds of research and development projects might be considered here. We have noted that the employment of EDP in education has been retarded by educators' negative attitudes toward and limited knowledge of automation. Actually, we know very little about either the prevalence of these unfortunate limitations or their specific nature. It is time that we found out precisely what exists in order to develop effective remedial measures.

Educators from time to time express fear that the incorporation of human programming errors into machine functioning will effect undetected injustices and inconveniences for students and teachers. How frequent and how serious are the errors now being committed by EDP? Do they go undetected? And how do the frequency and impact of errors with automated information processing compare with similar operations that are manually processed?

How have teacher roles been affected in schools or school districts now making extensive use of automation? There have been many speculations regarding the prospect of changed teacher functioning, most of them predicting that teachers will be freed for more appropriately human tasks. But data regarding what is actually happening are conspicuous by their absence.

Not only do we need answers to these and other questions but, in addition, there is urgent need for demonstration projects of many kinds, especially projects in secure or controlled situations that permit the admission of shortcomings or even of failures outweighing successes. The effective exploitation of trial situations suggests the need for temporary assignment of competent EDP analysts to them. Nothing quite equals demonstrations, when accompanied by the frank admission of shortcomings as well as assets, for giving the skeptical or ill-informed a sound basis for re-examining views that otherwise might soon petrify.

Conclusion

The essence of our findings and point of view toward the application of EDP in education are set forth in the following statements.

1. *No further research needs to be directed toward answering the question of whether it is practical and useful to apply automation to the solution of educational data processing problems.* Education is essentially an information processing enterprise in that huge masses of information are essential to its management and, for that matter, to the processes of inquiry that make up good teaching and learning.

2. *The field of education is still primitive in its use of EDP for those mass procedures pertaining to personnel, budget, facilities, and materials in which business, industry, and the military already have effectively demonstrated the benefits in economy and efficiency.* Some of the problems are economic: the problem of financing initial cost as well as the difficulty of computing gains in efficiency and personnel redevelopment in relation to input factors. But most of the problems lie in the realm of understanding and communication, especially at management levels.

3. *The most formidable block to progress in educational applications of EDP is not the state of the data processing art but our understanding of education as it presently operates and is likely to advance, especially our insight into the relationship between the human beings involved and the vast accumulation of organizational, instructional, and various ad hoc techniques that presently constitute our education system.* Part of this difficulty relates, in turn, to the crazy-quilt pattern of school district organization in America. Witness, for example, the data processing dilemmas involved in coordinating the information system of a secondary school with those of the six elementary schools supplying children from three independent school districts! The difficulties are further compounded when four of these elementary schools are traditional

in procedures and two represent the latest in classroom organization, curriculum content, and instructional innovations.

4. *There is a growing need for a "literature of experience" providing blow-by-blow accounts of how forward-looking states and school districts have resolved these difficulties of relationships and other problems in setting up automated school information processing systems.* Success stories alone are not enough. Unfortunately, it has always been difficult in education to ferret out information about potentially useful ventures that fail. Too many school leaders, after the arduous labors of convincing their boards and explaining their plans to the public, conclude that any subsequent failure simply must not be admitted.

5. *There is a communications gap between educators in schools, colleges, and universities who are strategic to the ultimate utilization of EDP in education and those specialists—EDP technologists and information scientists—who are professionally involved in the theory and practice of automated information processing.* Conferences for these two groups, deliberately designed to study the problems of applying EDP to education, will help, as will the mutual provision of opportunities to become more closely involved in each other's work. Both groups must exercise profound patience in struggling with differences in viewpoint and the semantic difficulties encountered in seeking to clarify these differences. But the phenomena of education are sufficiently challenging and provocative to bring able information scientists into needed research and development as avenues of communication increasingly open up.

6. *The most promising channels for research and development in educational EDP lie in determining those basic items of information that might constitute cooperative data processing systems, in standardizing nomenclature and definitions, in providing for system and subsystem compatibility, in resolving the interface problems between educational processes and technological processes (including the training of personnel to effect this interface), in investigating the potentiality of automation as an aid to educational innovation and experimentation, in studying and effecting instructional decisions, and in demonstrating tested procedures*

103

that might serve as models. These possibilities suggest tremendous geographic spread—from a single local school to a cooperative venture possibly embracing many states—and an equally great spread in the amount of data potentially involved. But grant funds must not be distributed according to the physical size of the educational units or the volume of data to be processed. Some small experimental projects can be enormously difficult, expensive, and significant.

7. *Fund granting agencies, in considering requests for financial support, are urged to look for the significance of a given project to education, its relevance to a wide range of applications, its possibilities in removing persistent roadblocks, its possibilities for dissemination and replication, its potentially cumulative contributions to knowledge, its possibilities for maximizing scarce resources, its provisions for field-testing, its contributions to efficiency, and its possibilities for self-sustainment.* This is by no means an exhaustive list. Nor are such criteria meaningful apart from the specific substance of recommendations for research and development such as those presented in this report. Taken together, however, these criteria and recommendations may prove helpful in deciding among proposals.

8. *Fears that automation will bring into education the anonymity and dehumanization now apparent in many aspects of daily life— even fear of the manipulation of individuals by robots—exist in many minds. Such fears must be reckoned with.* They are not new in civilization. To dispel them, man must look inside himself, not inside the computers. The computer has no mechanism of self-interest; man does. And so it is to the passions, inflexibility, and ignorance of man that we must look for the realization of our fears, just as we must look to his selflessness, adaptability, and wisdom for the fulfillment of our dreams.

In a special issue devoted to the triumphs and tragedies of the twentieth century, *Look* magazine [2] succinctly summarizes the fear ". . . that modern business will, in ruthless use of its brave new tools, bring a forced idleness for millions and a whole new

[2] January 12, 1965.

variety of inhumanities," and the hope that "the system that we are shaping, and that is shaping us, does more than pile up an abundance of goods. We seem to be driving ourselves, at electron speed, toward a society in which robots are the slaves, and man works at the difficult arts of civilization. If so, America may at last build what it promised itself 178 years ago: a nation in which each sovereign citizen pursues to the limit his human potential."

Viewed pessimistically or optimistically, the kind of world in which we are to live is to be a significantly automated one in which much of education too will be automated. But the essence of education that truly sets the spirit free promises to be so essentially human, individual, and elusive as to defy all efforts to translate it into terms that can be determined by computers.

Appendix A

Participants
of the
Lake Arrowhead
Conference

BARR, JOHN, Professor of Education, San Jose State College, San Jose, California.

BICKNELL, JOHN E., Director of Research, State Department of Education, St. Paul, Minnesota.

BOYER, E. GILL, Administrator, New England Educational Data Systems, 38 Kirkland Street, Cambridge, Massachusetts.

BOYER, ROSCOE A., Professor of Education, University of Mississippi, University, Mississippi.

BRADFORD, CLARENCE, Research Associate, Department of Education, University of Chicago, Illinois.

BUSHNELL, DAVID, Social Psychologist, Stanford Research Institute, Menlo Park, California.

BUSHNELL, DON D., Human Factors Scientist, System Development Corporation, 2500 Colorado Avenue, Santa Monica, California.

CAFFREY, JOHN G., Manager, Education Projects, System Development Corporation, 2500 Colorado Avenue, Santa Monica, California.

CONVERSE, FRED L., Human Factors Scientist, System Development Corporation, 2500 Colorado Avenue, Santa Monica, California.

FLERCHINGER, FRANCIS, Supervisor of Educational Records Systems, Office Superintendent of Public Instruction, State Department of Education, Olympia, Washington.

GATES, ROBERT, NDEA Coordinator, Florida State Department of Education, Tallahassee, Florida.

GOODLAD, JOHN I., Professor of Education and Director, University Elementary School, University of California, Los Angeles, California.

GOTLIEB, CALVIN, Director, Institute of Computer Science, University of Toronto, Ontario, Canada.

GROSSMAN, ALVIN, Director of Research and Development in Educational Data Processing Systems Project, State Department of Education, 721 Capitol Avenue, Sacramento, California.

GRUMAN, ALLEN J., Director of Data Processing, Sequoia Union High School District, 480 James Avenue, Redwood City, California.

HAMBLEN, JOHN W., Director, Data Processing and Computing Center, Southern Illinois University, Carbondale, Illinois.

HENDRIX, VERNON L., Assistant Professor of Education, University of California, Los Angeles, California.

HEWES, ROBERT E., Registrar, Massachusetts Institute of Technology, Cambridge, Massachusetts.

HOLLIS, ERNEST V., Director of College and University Administration, U.S. Office of Education, Division of Higher Education, Federal Office Building 6, Washington, D.C.

HUSEK, THEODORE R., Assistant Professor of Education, University of California, Los Angeles, California.

MC GRAW, PETER P., Specialist, Educational Data Systems, U.S. Office of Education, 400 Maryland Avenue, Washington, D.C.

MC PHEE, RODERICK F., Assistant Professor of Education, Graduate School of Education, Harvard University, Cambridge, Massachusetts.

MALLARY, NELSON D., JR., Director, Data Processing, State Department of Education, Atlanta, Georgia.

MORRISON, DON F., Assistant Professor, Texas A & M University, College Station, Texas.

O'TOOLE, JOHN F., JR., Assistant Manager, Education Projects, System Development Corporation, 2500 Colorado Avenue, Santa Monica, California.

PATTON, STANLEY R., Director of Data Processing, Chicago Board of Education, 228 North LaSalle, Chicago, Illinois.

PFEFERMAN, MURRAY, Coordinator, Systems Research and Development, U.S. Office of Education, Division of Educational Statistics, Federal Office Building 6, Washington, D.C.

PULLEN, CHARLES K., Chairman, Committee on Educational Data Systems, Council of Chief State School Officers, 113 Cordell Hull Building, Nashville, Tennessee.

ROBINSON, WADE M., Executive Director, School and University Program for Research and Development, Graduate School of Education, Harvard University, and Executive Director, Harvard University Committee on Programmed Instruction, 38 Kirkland Street, Cambridge, Massachusetts.

SNIDER, ROBERT, Assistant Executive Secretary, Department of Audio-Visual Instruction, National Education Association, 1201 16th Street, N.W., Washington, D.C.

STOTT, STERLING, Human Factors Scientist, System Development Corporation, 2500 Colorado Avenue, Santa Monica, California.

SULLIVAN, JOHN W., Professor, School of Business Administration, Wayne State University, Detroit, Michigan.

TASHNOVIAN, PETER, Consultant in Education Research, State Department of Education, 721 Capitol Avenue, Sacramento, California.

THAYER, ARTHUR N., Assistant Coordinator, Program on the Education of Teachers, University of California, Los Angeles, California.

TONDOW, MURRAY, Director of Pupil Personnel Services, Palo Alto Unified School District, 25 Churchill Avenue, Palo Alto, California.

WALKER, VIRGIL R., Acting Director, Division of Educational Statistics, U.S. Office of Education, Federal Office Building 6, Washington, D.C.

WALTON, WESLEY W., Director, Developmental Programs, Educational Testing Service, Princeton, New Jersey.

Descriptions of State, Regional, and Local Educational Data Processing Programs

This Appendix indicates not only the great diversity of problems and solutions in educational data processing but the many common factors among these school programs. The twenty-seven educational agencies and institutions described in this Appendix represent a broad cross section of data processing programs, varying widely in the sophistication and size of the hardware used as well as in the size and political level of the populations served. Implementation in school districts and state education agencies range from a multi-computer configuration with a million-dollar annual budget to a center with no equipment whose annual budget of a few hundred dollars pays for the use of a small installation in a nearby community. The populations served range from a state serving sixteen hundred school districts to a school district with only seven thousand pupils. In Table 3, each institution in this Appendix is categorized according to the size of the population served and the size of the hardware configuration used.

In many cases, the reader might well ask why a particular system or institution is mentioned and so many others are omitted. This appendix attempts only to sample and to provide specific leads for further inquiry. The institutions presented were chosen in part to represent a variety of geographic regions—from Washington to Florida, from California to Massachusetts, and from Alaska to Hawaii. Many outstanding data processing programs and systems were omitted because descriptions of them would have been merely

111

duplication. The reader in need of further examples might consult Luton Reed's *Data Processing Systems* (see Appendix C), which presents statistics for 165 institutions.

The data presented here have been volunteered in all cases by individuals currently familiar with the status of data processing in the institution reported. In no case are such data older than August 1964, although for some institutions financial data were available only for a prior fiscal year. Since that time, many of the listed school districts and state departments have broadened the scope of their EDP operations, increased personnel, expanded budget allocations to handle new computing equipment and other hardware, and implemented new systems. These data should therefore be used cautiously, since EDP is obviously a rapidly growing enterprise in education, and extrapolations must be made in order to estimate the current situation.

Figures for budgeted expenditures are included for each district, county, or state to indicate its size and to provide a basis for meaningful comparisons of the other financial data. Budget figures represent expenditures from current income only (including debt retirement) and exclude funds from increases in indebtedness such as the sale of bonds. Local (district or county) budget figures represent the total expenditures at that level paid for by funds from all sources, including state and federal aid. Two figures are given for each state budget: "state income" represents expenditures paid for by taxes generated by the state. "All sources" represents expenditures paid for by state taxes plus federal aid to education. All figures for total expenditures include expenditures for data processing and for hardware rental and maintenance.

The figures for "data processing" or for specific data centers represent the annual cost of processing data: payments for salaries, training programs, materials, labor, etc. to operate the institution's equipment and/or payments to outside service bureaus.

"Hardware" includes all computer and punched card equipment that encodes or processes data from machine sensible documents. Not included are equipment for handling forms, bursters, decollators, bundle tying machines, paper cutters, and printing presses. Typewriters are included only if specially obtained as input to character recognition systems. "Hardware owned" excludes items not ordinarily capitalized, such as control panels for leased machines. Figures for hardware owned or for computers owned represent the cost of equipment at installation. Figures for "hardware rental and maintenance" are separate from the figures for hardware owned and the figures for data processing or data centers.

Hardware manufacturers are indicated by the following abbreviations plus the appropriate model numbers:

> B—Burroughs Corporation
> CDC—Control Data Corporation
> GE—General Electric Corporation
> H—Minneapolis Honeywell Regulator Company
> IBM—International Business Machines Corporation
> NCR—National Cash Register Company
> RCA—Radio Corporation of America
> SDS—Scientific Data Systems
> U—Univac Division of Sperry Rand Corporation

In data processing for public education, factors such as personnel, hardware, software, and money do not stand still for a portrait. We merely present some snapshots. The utility of publishing a more comprehensive directory every year or two is apparent, and we hope this collection of sample descriptions may provide the nucleus of such an effort.

TABLE 3

Institutions According to Size of Equipment Configuration and Population Served

Political level and size of population served	SIZE OF HARDWARE CONFIGURATION USED		
	Medium, large or multiple computer system used substantially	*Small, computer in house, little out-of-house usage*	*No computer in house, punched card oriented*
State departments of education	13, 15	8, 22	11, 14, 19
Regional service centers	21	6	5
Counties	7	17	12, 16
Very large districts (100,000 pupils or more)	9	3	10, 14
Large districts (30,000 to less than 100,000)	18	24	26
Medium districts (10,000 to less than 30,000)		23	1, 2, 4
Small districts (less than 10,000)		25	20, 27

Each entry in the above table represents one of the institutions listed below:

1. Anchorage Independent School District, Alaska
2. Ann Arbor Public Schools, Michigan
3. Baltimore Public Schools, Maryland
4. Bellevue Public Schools (District 405), Washington
5. Broward County Board of Public Instruction, Florida
6. California State Department of Education
7. Cayuga County Board of Cooperative Educational Services, New York
8. Chicago Public Schools, Illinois
9. Cleveland Public Schools, Ohio

114

10. Connecticut State Department of Education
11. Dougherty County Public Schools, Georgia
12. Florida State Department of Education
13. Gateway Union School District, Pennsylvania
14. Hawaii State Department of Education
15. Iowa Educational Information Center
16. Jefferson County Public Schools, Kentucky
17. Jefferson County School District R-1, Colorado
18. Los Angeles Junior College District, California
19. Massachusetts State Department of Education
20. New England Education Data Systems, Cambridge, Massachusetts
21. New York State Department of Education, SUNY
22. Palo Alto Unified School District, California
23. Rochester Public Schools, New York
24. Shaker Heights Public Schools, Ohio
25. Tulsa County Independent School District 1, Oklahoma
26. Ventura Union High School District, California
27. Westchester County Board of Cooperative Educational Services (Second Supervisory District), New York

1

ANCHORAGE INDEPENDENT SCHOOL DISTRICT
Anchorage, Alaska

18,000 pupils, K–12, plus community college
Punched card equipment acquired in 1960 [1]
Approximate budgeted expenditures for fiscal 1965:
   For district $13,000,000
      For data processing $54,000
      For hardware rental and maintenance   not available
Computers owned: none

Anchorage has a punched card machine installation (IBM Series 50) which is thus far used primarily for general business and student accounting applications. A local service bureau with a computer (IBM-1620) is being utilized for class scheduling. Plans are now being coordinated with the Alaska state government for a program of staff accounting, with directory information being processed first, as a tie-in

[1] Throughout the tabular material, "acquired" includes equipment either leased or owned.

115

to certification, payroll, etc. Tremendous growth in data processing services is expected by the administration.

The staff of 4 includes a data processing supervisor, a tab operator, and 2 keypunch operators. The Controller, Jerry N. Waddell, is responsible for systems planning, development, and operations, and reports to the Assistant Superintendent for Administration, Don E. Fridley. The Superintendent is Don M. Dafoe.

2

ANN ARBOR PUBLIC SCHOOLS
Ann Arbor, Michigan

15,000 pupils, K–12
Punched card equipment acquired in 1962
Approximate budgeted expenditures for fiscal 1964:

For district		$9,197,925
For Data Center	$40,000	
For hardware rental and maintenance	15,000	

Computers owned: none

Ann Arbor's machine installation includes a calculating punch (IBM-602), an accounting machine (IBM-402), a reproducer, a collator, an interpreter, a sorter, a keypunch, and a verifier. One high school also has a document writer (IBM-826) with a keypunch and a sorter. Principal applications are payroll, accounts payable, accounts receivable, financial statistics, census, scheduling, grade reporting and cumulative records. The high school equipment is used in attendance accounting.

The staff of 3 in the Data Center is led by David Classon, Supervisor of Data Processing, who reports through Gerald Neff, Assistant Superintendent, to Jack Elzay, Superintendent.

116

3

BALTIMORE PUBLIC SCHOOLS
Baltimore, Maryland

196,000 pupils, K–12, plus 2,100 junior college students
Punched card equipment acquired in 1928; computer configuration acquired in 1964
Approximate budgeted expenditures for fiscal 1965:

For district		$105,000,000
For Data Processing Center (excluding testing)	$154,000	
For hardware rental and maintenance	55,000	

Hardware owned: $471,000

The Baltimore school system has a basic punched card machine installation as support for a computer (IBM-1401 16K) with 4 tape drives and 2 disc drives. The basic equipment consists of an accounting machine (IBM-407), 2 collators, several reproducers, an interpreter, a sorter, several keypunches, and a verifier. The junior college also has a computer (IBM-1620).

The Data Processing Center is used for instruction in computer programming, computer operation, computer repair, and for both secondary and adult education classes. It is also used for instruction in mathematics, science, and business education. The Data Processing Center's services include inventory control, payroll and cost analyses, report cards, pupil attendance, test scoring, and budget preparation.

The Data Processing Center is under the immediate supervision of the Director of Research, Orlando F. Furno. Edward W. Riedel is Special Assistant to the Director and Data Processing Manager; Carroll Lloyd is Acting Head of Systems and Programming Procedures; Martin H. Raila is concerned with Systems Analysis Procedures. The staff involved in data processing and systems work includes 13 persons in the Data Center proper and 6 persons in systems and programming work.

4

BELLEVUE PUBLIC SCHOOLS (DISTRICT 405)
Bellevue, Washington

17,600 pupils, K–12
Punched card operations begun in 1960
Approximate budgeted expenditures for fiscal 1965:

For district		$9,500,000
For Data Processing Center	$30,000	
For hardware rental and maintenance	12,000	

Hardware owned: $1,000

The Data Processing Center has an accounting machine (IBM-402), a reproducer, a collator, an interpreter, 2 sorters, a keypunch, and a verifier. This equipment services 10 secondary schools, 19 elementary schools, business and administrative divisions and such special areas as testing.

Services for all schools include: (1) a federal aid survey (Public Law 874, U.S. Congress), student accident reports, student residence zones, testing, guidance, a physical fitness survey of students, class lists, physical education records, attendance and research, a textbooks list; (2) junior and senior high school student class lists, scheduling, report cards, failure and incomplete lists, address files, GPA computations, GPA lists alphabetical and by rank, and student body accounting; (3) in the business division, payroll time sheets, computing of payroll, payroll reports for certificated and classified, FICA reports, withholding statements, labor distribution, job cost, inventory, employee monthly audits, employee ledger posting, address labels, industrial arts and textbook order forms; (4) personnel accounting, summer school scheduling, class lists, and bus routes and stops. At the present time, systems analysis is being done by the staff to integrate the personnel and payroll departments. Also, systems analysis is presently directed towards purchasing, accounts payable, and cost accounting.

A staff of 3 assists Alanson T. Powell, Business Manager, who reports to Myron Ernst, Superintendent.

5

BROWARD COUNTY BOARD OF PUBLIC INSTRUCTION (BPI)
Fort Lauderdale, Florida

81,000 pupils, K–14
Punched card operations begun in 1959; computer acquired in 1963
Approximate budgeted expenditures for fiscal 1965:
For Board of Public Instruction $36,500,000
   For data processing $250,000
   For hardware rental and maintenance   165,000
Computers owned: none

Broward County BPI has 2 computers (IBM-1620 20K, IBM-1401 8K column binary) with 2 magnetic tape drives and 2 magnetic disc drives. There is telephonic data transmission equipment connecting the Computer Center at the Junior College with the BPI office. The complete line of supporting equipment includes 2 accounting machines (IBM-407 and IBM-402) and 27 keypunches. Keypunches are installed in 19 schools; sorters are installed in 8.

Pupil record applications are of special interest: student schedules, teacher schedules, class rolls, locator cards, welfare and attendance cards, library labels, grade audit sheets, report cards, class loads, permanent record labels, GPA reports, grade distributions, locker assignments, bus rosters, assembly seat assignments, and graduation lists. Magnetic disc pack procedures for permanent records and for assigning students to course sections are being tested.

In addition to pupil records, substantial service is offered in 8 areas: payroll and personnel, accounting, testing pupil accounting, instruction (data processing and computer technology), budget analysis and control, data transmission, and systems design. The center has cooperated in developmental work on significant innovations for Nova High School and for Florida Atlantic University.

A central staff of 16, headed by the Director of Data Processing, works closely with the junior college data processing laboratory staff of 5 and with the operators at 19 schools. Included are 2 programmers, a systems analyst, and a communications specialist. The Director, William J. English, reports to Myron L. Ashmore, Superintendent.

6

CALIFORNIA STATE DEPARTMENT OF EDUCATION
Sacramento, California

4,440,000 pupils, K–12 in 1,600 districts, plus junior colleges
Punched card equipment acquired in 1946; computer configuration acquired in 1962
Approximate budgeted expenditures for fiscal 1965:

For state from all sources		$3,500,000,000
From state income	$1,385,000,000	
For Bureau of Educational Research		300,000
For hardware rental and maintenance		22,000

Hardware owned: $500,000

The Bureau of Educational Research has a computer (RCA-301 20K) with 6 magnetic tape drives, a printer, a card reader and a punch. Support is provided by a basic machine installation including a tabulator (IBM-402). The unit serves the entire Department in all phases of its data processing needs.

The installation is responsible for the computation of all school apportionments, which amounted to $850,000,000 in 1964–65; the analysis of state test data for 800,000 pupils; analysis of financial transactions of school districts; distribution of textbooks; surveys of school enrollments and salaries; school lunch and surplus property programs; vocational education programs; property accounting; and a large and varied number of special projects and services.

The staff consists of a consultant in education research, a data processing manager, 1 ATMS II supervisor, 4 programmers, a console operator, 2 tab operators, and 10 keypunch operators. Consultant Peter J. Tashnovian is responsible for the operation of the installation.

7

CAYUGA COUNTY BOARD OF COOPERATIVE EDUCATIONAL
SERVICES (BOCES)
Auburn, New York

7,000 pupils, K–12, in 6 central school districts
Punched card equipment acquired in 1964
Approximate budgeted expenditures for fiscal 1965:
For BOCES		$300,000
For data processing	$19,000	
For hardware rental and maintenance	not available	
Computers owned: none

Cayuga County BOCES leases an accounting machine (IBM-402) supported by a reproducer (IBM-514), a sorter, and (located in the participating schools) 4 keypunches. The immediate task is the service of 6 central districts, but it is hoped that in the spring costs will be reduced by renting equipment to other nearby districts. The center will be used for attendance accounting and the production of report cards. It will also be used for instruction in business education.

The center presently has a staff of 1, the supervising operator, Frederick Scholl, who reports to Raymond T. Sant, District Superintendent. The participating school districts employ 2 part-time and 2 full-time keypunch operators.

8

CHICAGO PUBLIC SCHOOLS
Chicago, Illinois

600,000 pupils, K–16
Punched card equipment acquired about 1935; computer configuration acquired in 1963
Approximate budgeted expenditures for fiscal 1965:
For district		$325,000,000
For Bureau of Data Processing	$1,100,000	
For hardware rental and maintenance	400,000	
Computers owned: none

The Bureau of Data Processing has an optical character-recognition data converter with an attached computer (SDS-910 8K) and 2 tape

121

drives. This equipment was designed to read both typewritten copy and computer-printed copy. The magnetic tapes from the data converter are expected to constitute the principal data input to the Bureau's computer complex (IBM-7074 10K, 2 IBM-1401 8K, and a 1401 4K). Altogether there are 18 tape drives attached. The complete line of supporting punched card equipment includes 15 keypunches. The installation is used to implement a "Total Information Service" integrating data processing services in 6 areas: budget and finance, personnel and payroll, materials, student accounting and scheduling, computer education, and research.

The staff of 83 includes 35 systems analysts and programmers and is divided into 4 principal groups led by L. Lafave (Data Processing Education), H. Levine (Research), J. Clancy (Operations), and R. Baileys (Systems). J. Quinn, Assistant Director, Administration, reports to Stanley R. Patton, Director of Data Processing, who reports to James F. Redmond, General Superintendent of Schools.

9

CLEVELAND PUBLIC SCHOOLS
Cleveland, Ohio

154,000 pupils, K–12
Punched card equipment acquired in 1962
Approximate budgeted expenditures for fiscal 1964:

For district		$64,000,000
For Data Center	$40,000	
For outside data processing services	9,000	
For hardware rental and maintenance	15,000	

Computers owned: none

Cleveland has 2 data processing installations, 1 under the control of the Superintendent and 1 under the control of the Clerk-Treasurer (reporting directly to the Board). A small computer is now on order and a larger computer planned for the future is expected to serve all areas and thus lead to the elimination of separate installations. At present the 2 accounting machines (IBM-403) and supporting punched card equipment are devoted to financial accounting, textbook ordering and distribution, certificated personnel records, scheduling, grade reporting, and such by-products as class ranks. Scheduling is done with the help of a computer (IBM-7090), which is available through a service bureau.

In one data processing installation a staff of 3, plus 1 part-time person, assists Darien Smith, Assistant Superintendent, Personnel, who reports through A. R. Dittrick, Deputy Superintendent to Paul Briggs, Superintendent. In the other installation, a staff of 3 reports to Michael Wach, Clerk-Treasurer.

10

CONNECTICUT STATE DEPARTMENT OF EDUCATION
Hartford, Connecticut

Size and grade level of pupil population not available
Punched card operations begun in 1961
Approximate budgeted expenditures for fiscal 1963:

For state from all sources		$288,500,000
From state income	$102,100,000	
For data processing	22,000	
For hardware rental and mainte- nance	4,000	

Hardware owned: $3,000

The Connecticut State Department of Education has a small punched card installation, including an accounting machine (IBM-402 Series 50), a sorter, 2 keypunches, and a verifier. Service is provided for application-grant payment, registration of certificated personnel, salary studies, teacher demand, school population, physical education, and school milk and lunch programs. Some of these applications require use of an all-alphabetic printer (IBM-407) or of a small computer (IBM-1620, 1401, and 1440), access to which is provided by Connecticut State Technical Institute.

The staff is composed of 3 persons, headed by Herbert Hill, Senior Tab Supervisor, who reports through Maurice Ross, Chief, Bureau of Statistics, to William J. Sanders, Commissioner.

11

DOUGHERTY COUNTY PUBLIC SCHOOLS
Albany, Georgia

21,000 pupils, 1–12
Punched card operations begun in 1963
Approximate budgeted expenditures for fiscal 1965:

For district		$6,100,000
For Data Center	$35,000	
For hardware rental	15,000	

Computers owned: none

Dougherty County has an optical scanner (IBM-1232) with an attached punch, a tabulator (IBM-407), a reproducer, a collator, a sorter, and 2 keypunches. The equipment is used in payroll and in maintaining a file of student registration data. The scanner is used in attendance accounting. Additional equipment in the area vocational school is used in an adult program.

A supervising operator, 2 keypunch operators and temporary help report to J. G. Sowell, Business Manager, who reports to J. J. Cordell, Superintendent.

12

FLORIDA STATE DEPARTMENT OF EDUCATION
Tallahassee, Florida

1,200,000 pupils, in 67 school districts
Punched card operations begun in 1939; acquired punched card equipment in 1960 and a computer in 1962
Approximate budgeted expenditures for fiscal 1964:

For state from all sources (including local)		$496,000,000
From state income	$273,000,000	
For data processing	305,000	
For hardware and rental maintenance	130,000	

Hardware owned: $394,000

The Department of Education has 2 computer systems (IBM-1401 8K and RCA-301 20K) with 11 magnetic tape drives supported by a

7 keypunch EAM installation that includes a statistical sorter (IBM-101). The installation is used to summarize data from the local districts, to process personnel records, and to produce financial reports and reports of special education. Substantial effort has been devoted to the development of a library of programs of use to the local districts.

The staff of 36 includes L. Everett Yarbrough, Systems Consultant; Archie B. Johnston, Systems Consultant; Robert W. Sims, Coordinator of Systems; A. Buford Moulton, Coordinator of Data Processing. The system is under the direction of James K. Chapman, Deputy Superintendent, who reports to Thomas D. Bailey, Superintendent.

13

GATEWAY UNION SCHOOL DISTRICT
Monroeville, Pennsylvania

7,400 pupils, 1–12
Punched card operations begun in 1962
Approximate budgeted expenditures for fiscal 1965:
For district		$4,500,000
For outside data processing services	$2,000	
For hardware rental and maintenance	none	

Hardware owned: none

Gateway uses equipment owned by Allegheny County, housed at Forbes Trail School, and used primarily in an area vocational training program. Scheduling, report cards, and attendance accounting are present applications. Consideration is being given to use in financial accounting.

The efforts of county personnel, students, graduates of the vocational program, and regular clerical employees are used as needed under the coordination of Eugene B. Yarnell, High School Principal, who reports to Carl Newman, Superintendent.

14

HAWAII STATE DEPARTMENT OF EDUCATION
Honolulu, Hawaii

176,000 pupils, K–adult
Punched card equipment acquired in 1960
Approximate budgeted expenditures for fiscal 1964:

For state from all sources		$59,000,000
From state income	$53,000,000	
For data processing	140,000	
For hardware rental and maintenance	40,000	

Computers owned: none

The Hawaii State Department of Education is unique in that it operates the local schools of the state and also performs the usual state functions. The Office of Research, Statistics, and Data Processing has 2 accounting machines (IBM-407) supported by 2 reproducers, an interpreter, a collator, 2 sorters, 2 test scoring machines, and 5 keypunches.

Major application areas include the following: budget and appropriation accounting, staff personnel accounting, cafeteria accounting, library order processing, student master records, student scheduling, grade reporting and analysis, test scoring and analysis, institutional and educational research, and service to 3 other state departments for miscellaneous applications.

The department is presently using the University of Hawaii's computer (IBM-1401, with tapes), for the processing and analysis of pupil test data, and for research projects and personnel applications. Programming and processing include some personnel accounting on the IBM-1401. Planning for a computer-based total information system has begun.

Superintendent of Public Instruction is R. Burl Yarberry. Assistant Superintendent for Research, Statistics, and Data Processing is William G. Savard. Data Processing Unit Supervisor is Tad T. Nakano. The staff includes a computer programmer, 4 tabulating equipment operators, a keypunch supervisor, 7 keypunch operators, a test scoring supervising clerk, and 2 part-time clerks.

15

IOWA EDUCATIONAL INFORMATION CENTER
Iowa City, Iowa

620,000 pupils, K–12, in 2,000 school districts
Punched card and computer operations begun in 1962
Approximate budgeted expenditures for fiscal 1965:

For Information Center		$220,000
For computer and scanner utilization	$150,000	

Computers owned: none

The Information Center, a joint venture of the State Department of Public Instruction and the University of Iowa, now operates project UPDATE, which started on a limited scale in 1962–63 and began services under its present organization January 1, 1964. The Center is funded by an 18-month grant from the U.S. Office of Education for almost $250,000 and a 5-year grant from the Ford Foundation for $750,000. The Center serves the entire state and some out-of-state school districts in 3 areas: educational specifications, systems and procedures, and field operations (where it is concerned with data gathering, system design and maintenance, and information dissemination).

Actual processing, however, is done through the Measurement Research Center on its optical scanner and 2 computers (CDC-160 and IBM-1460). Substantial work is also done at the University Computing Center (IBM-7040). The State Department of Public Instruction maintains a punched card installation at Des Moines for preparing input both to the Information Center and to the open shop State Computer Center under the administration of the State Controller.

Applications make use of highly sophisticated techniques and hardware to exploit the entire range of educational data. Computer class sectioning has already been applied to 60 high schools. Magnetic tapes are being prepared with unit records of every child in the state testing program. The Center also has a program of instruction for doctoral candidates in education who wish to specialize in data processing.

The staff of 19 is led by Robert Marker, Director; Ralph Van Dusseldorp, Associate Director; Bruce Alcorn, Program Coordinator; and Peter McGraw, Assistant Director for Program Development. The Department of Public Instruction's Data Center at Des Moines is under the direction of Marvin Ingle. The State Computer Center is under the administration of Harold Gandy, Controller.

16

JEFFERSON COUNTY PUBLIC SCHOOLS
Louisville, Kentucky

67,000 pupils, 1–12
Computer configuration acquired in 1960
Approximate budgeted expenditures for fiscal 1965:

For district		$25,000,000
For data processing	$60,000	
For hardware rental	25,000	

Computers owned: none

The Jefferson County office serves the schools in the county system but does not serve independent schools. Louisville leases an installation for its own use. The county equipment includes a computer (NCR-390) with an on-line keypunch, a typewriter, a paper tape reader and punch, and an accounting machine (NCR-31) with additional paper tape output. Off-line support includes 2 keypunches and a sorter. The equipment not only handles paper tape and punched cards but also NCR ledger cards storing up to 200 characters in magnetic strips. Principal applications are in the areas of census, budget, purchase order control, payroll, attendance accounting, and professional personnel records.

For data processing there is a staff of 4, plus 1 part-time person, in the business area and a staff of 3 in the census area; both staffs report to E. Grayson, Associate Superintendent for Accounting and Finance, who reports to Richard Van Hoose, Superintendent.

17

JEFFERSON COUNTY SCHOOL DISTRICT R-1
Jefferson County, Colorado

50,000 pupils, K–12, plus special education and adult education courses
Punched card equipment acquired in 1959
Approximate budgeted expenditures for calendar 1965:

For district		$27,000,000
For information services (excluding testing)	$70,000	
For hardware rental and maintenance	26,000	

Computers owned: none

Jefferson County School District R-1 has a unit-record installation consisting of 2 accounting machines (IBM-403), an interpreter (IBM-557), and a complete line of supporting punched card equipment.

The unit-record equipment is used for instruction in business education. Computer time is "begged, borrowed, and bought" for instruction in mathematics and science. Business services include payroll, accounts payable, directories, property accounting, and label addressing. Educational services include student scheduling (4 schools have been scheduled for 1964–65 on an IBM-1620), attendance reporting, grade reporting, permanent record labels, certificated personnel statistics, and some local test analysis.

The staff of 7 includes 4 punch operators, 2 tab operators, and a data processing supervisor. Supervisor Murry C. Grigsby reports to the Director of Research, Edward Brainard, who in turn reports to the Superintendent of Schools, Forbes Bottomly.

18

LOS ANGELES JUNIOR COLLEGE DISTRICT
Los Angeles, California

70,600 students, 13–14

Punched card equipment acquired in 1949; computer configuration acquired in 1957

Approximate budgeted expenditures for fiscal 1964:

For district		$23,000,000
For data processing	not available	
For hardware rental and maintenance	$100,000	

Hardware owned: $540,000

There are 7 colleges in this district. Six have EAM units, used primarily for administrative work, assigned to the admissions offices. Instructional demonstrations are also given from time to time during the semester. Eight small computers (7 IBM-1620's and 1 CDC G-15) are installed at 6 of the colleges. These are used primarily for instruction in mathematics, business, and electronics technician training.

The EAM units are staffed by a supervisor, from 1 to 4 machine operators, and a keypunch operator. The computers are staffed by members of the instructional departments involved and by various lab assistants. Administrative work done on the computers is the responsibility of the staffs of the EAM units. All 7 colleges are directed by the

Assistant Superintendent, Walter Coultas, who reports to the Associate Superintendent of College and Adult Education, T. Stanley Warburton, who in turn reports to the Superintendent of Schools, Jack P. Crowther. A Data Processing Coordinator for the 7 colleges, Lloyd Cadbury, reports to Coultas.

19

MASSACHUSETTS STATE DEPARTMENT OF EDUCATION
Boston, Massachusetts

926,000 pupils, K–12, in 387 districts
Punched card equipment acquired in 1960
Approximate budgeted expenditures for fiscal 1963:

For state from all sources		$401,500,000
From state income	$97,000,000	
For Division of Research and Statistics	100,000	
For hardware rental	20,000	

Hardware owned: $13,500

The Division of Research and Statistics has a tabulator (IBM-407), supported by a reproducer, a collator, an interpreter, a sorter, 4 keypunches, and a verifier. The equipment is used primarily for the preparation of statistics under Title X of the National Defense Education Act. All divisions of the Department of Education are serviced by the data center. Considerable use is made of computer installations in the Boston area to develop programs for future use on a department computer. The Division has also been of service to the local school systems, helping them with pupil attendance and high school scheduling procedures.

A staff of 5 assists Glenn Myers, Supervisor, who reports to Raymond S. Dower, Jr., Director. Owen B. Kiernan is Commissioner of Education.

130

20

NEW ENGLAND EDUCATION DATA SYSTEMS (NEEDS)
Cambridge, Massachusetts

50,000 pupils, K–16, in 23 grade school and college systems
Computer configuration acquired in 1963
Approximate budgeted expenditures for fiscal 1964–65:

For NEEDS from all sources [2]		over $1,000,000
For central installation	$371,000	
For hardware rental and mainte- nance (central installation)	55,000	

Computers owned: none

NEEDS used borrowed hardware for several years to do developmental work and to offer experimental services to its members. When NEEDS acquired its own computer in 1963, it began to offer full services from its central installation. The NEEDS computer (IBM-1401 8K column binary) has 4 magnetic tape drives and 2 disc drives. A complete punched card installation includes an accounting machine (IBM-407) and 6 keypunches. NEEDS uses large computers (IBM-7090) at Harvard University and MIT as well. In addition, there are 3 satellite punched card installations in member districts. Newton, Massachusetts, and Manchester, Connecticut, have installations including a tabulator (IBM-407) and Danvers, Massachusetts, has a smaller installation (IBM-402).

A complete range of data processing services is offered to members, especially class sectioning and computerized assistance in master schedule building. The desired characteristics and potential uses of the data bank created as a by-product of the system are being studied by John B. Carroll, Professor of Education, Harvard University.

A staff of 20, plus 13 part-time students, is needed for administration, system development, and programming. Allan B. Ellis is in charge of basic research and formal instruction. Victor Oppenheimer is Acting Director of Operations. Both report to Gil Boyer, Administrator. The board of directors represents 6 state departments of education, member universities, and the New England School Development Council.

[2] This figure includes financial credits granted to member districts by NEEDS for its use of their services, machine rental, space, etc., and some financial support from the Ford Foundation.

21

NEW YORK STATE DEPARTMENT OF EDUCATION, SUNY
Albany, New York

4,200,000 pupils, K–16, in 1,300 school systems
Punched card operations begun about 1955; computer configuration
acquired in 1964
Approximate budgeted expenditures for fiscal 1964:

For state from all sources (including local)		$3,300,000,000
From state income	$1,336,000,000	
For Bureau of Electronic Data Processing		600,000
For hardware rental and maintenance		170,000

Computers owned: none

The Bureau of Electronic Data Processing has a computer (GE-225 8K) with 6 magnetic tape drives and an optical scanner (Digitek). A large EAM installation, including several accounting machines (IBM-407), calculating punches, and a keypunch-verifying section of about 20 machines, is being cut back somewhat now that the computer has been installed. The EAM equipment will continue many of the present applications in research and statistics, such as financial, attendance, and vocational rehabilitation reports. The first applications of the computer are the state scholarship program and the state registration of certain professionals such as certified public accountants, nurses, and teachers.

The Bureau's staff of about 45, with 2 systems analysts and 6 programmers, is headed by Ruth Callahan, Director of Data Processing, who reports through Ewald Nyquist, Associate Commissioner, to James E. Allen, Commissioner.

22

PALO ALTO UNIFIED SCHOOL DISTRICT
Palo Alto, California

15,000 pupils, K–12
Punched card equipment acquired in 1958, computer configuration acquired in 1963
Approximate budgeted expenditures for fiscal 1965:

For district		$11,000,000
For information services (including group testing)	$140,000	
For hardware rental and maintenance	33,000	

Hardware owned: $130,000

Palo Alto has an optical scanner (Franklin Chang) and a basic EAM installation as support for a small computer (IBM-1620) with magnetic disc storage and a line printer. The computer is used for instruction in programming for both secondary and adult classes, and for instruction in mathematics, science, and business education. Educational services include pupil scheduling, report cards, attendance system (including weekly reports to counselors), posting of transcripts, test scoring and data analysis, parent name and address label printing, personnel records, assistance with budget preparation, and a variety of specialized services.

A district-wide coordinating committee assists in establishing policies for system operation and in implementing new applications. Considerable use is made of available files for research and evaluation of the district's educational program. Occasional use is made of an out-of-house H-800, an IBM-7090, a B-200, and a CDC-1604.

The staff of 12 persons includes a system analyst, 2 project specialists, 2 programmers, a group testing supervisor, a computer center manager, and a second shift supervisor. The Director of Information Services, Murray Tondow, reports to the Superintendent of Schools, Harold Santee.

23

ROCHESTER PUBLIC SCHOOLS
Rochester, New York

46,000 pupils, K–12

Punched card equipment acquired in 1959; computer configuration acquired in 1964

Approximate budgeted expenditures for fiscal 1965:

For district		$31,000,000
For Data Center	$115,000	
For hardware rental	54,000	

Computers owned: none

Rochester's basic EAM installation is used for financial accounting (payroll, inventory, budget), student accounting (scheduling, report cards), and many other services. An optical scanner (IBM-1230) has been installed since March 1964, primarily for test scoring, but is also used in other applications. A B-263 computer was installed in October 1964, to replace 2 IBM-407's and an IBM-602, and a B-283 computer was recently acquired. Also, at one of the high schools, IBM Series 50 equipment has been installed for instruction.

The staff of 9 is headed by Data Processing Supervisor, Carl S. Florino. Paul Reason, Assistant Superintendent, in charge of Business Affairs reports to Herman Goldbert, Superintendent.

24

SHAKER HEIGHTS PUBLIC SCHOOLS
Shaker Heights, Ohio

7,600 pupils, K–12

Punched card equipment acquired in 1960; computer configuration acquired in 1965

Approximate budgeted expenditures for fiscal 1964:

For district		$6,700,000
For Data Center	$46,000	
For hardware rental	25,000	

Computers owned: none

Shaker Heights installed a computer (U-1004) in 1965. The installation also includes equipment installed before the computer—an optical

134

scanning punch (U-5340), an accounting machine (U-6090, Model 3), and supporting punched card machines.

Applications to date include student information services, report cards, attendance, cumulative records in the elementary school, test scoring and tabulating, student scheduling (primarily the printing of student schedules), master lists, class lists, employee absence, cumulative sick leave, substitute payroll, miscellaneous personnel information, including salary certification, and budget control reports. It is anticipated that the installation will eventually handle the full range of educational and business procedures. Plans are under way to institute instruction in data processing at the high school level.

The staff includes 3 operators and a data processing supervisor. The installation is under the direct supervision of William Cunningham, Assistant to the Superintendent, who reports to the Superintendent of Schools, Donald G. Emery.

25

TULSA COUNTY INDEPENDENT SCHOOL DISTRICT 1
Tulsa, Oklahoma

75,000 pupils, K–12
Punched card operations begun in 1963
Approximate budgeted expenditures for fiscal 1964:

For district	not available
For data processing	$65,000
For hardware rental	23,000

Computers owned: none

Tulsa has acquired an optical scanner (IBM-1230) with a punch. The installation includes a calculating punch (IBM-604), a tabulator (IBM-407), and a complete supporting EAM installation with 3 keypunches. Initial applications have been financial accounting (especially cafeteria and payroll for 3,500 employees), research, analysis and summarization of test data, census, and attendance.

The staff of 8 include J. O. Brown, Manager of the Data Processing Department, reporting to H. H. Edwards, Director of Attendance and Census, who reports through Cecil Benson, Assistant Superintendent, to Charles Mason, Superintendent.

135

26

VENTURA UNION HIGH SCHOOL DISTRICT
Ventura, California

6,500 pupils, 7–12
Punched card equipment acquired in 1958
Approximate budgeted expenditures for fiscal 1964–1965:

For district		$5,200,000
For Data Center	$41,000	
For outside data processing services	less than 300	
For hardware rental	17,000	

Computers owned: none

The Data Center has an accounting machine (IBM-407) supported by a reproducer, an interpreter, a collator, a sorter, and 2 keypunches. Out-of-house computers (IBM-1440, 1401, and 7044) are used during the school year for some business extensions, GPA reports, and registration of students. The Ventura County Schools Office scores all standardized tests. All other testing processes (labels, distributions, etc.) are accomplished in the District Data Center.

Student applications include registration, attendance accounting, roll books, grade reporting, testing, test reporting, transcripts, student voting, student body locker cards, athletic classification, master program building, curriculum studies, grouping studies, and parent communications of various types.

Business applications include appropriation ledgers, general ledgers, warehouse issue and control, accounts payable, warrants, payroll warrants, state retirement, social security, federal withholding statements, and budget and cafeteria reporting.

The high school business education department gives some instruction for business students. Each school has representatives on a district-wide data processing council. Every other year a handbook is published.

The staff includes a tab supervisor and 2 keypunch machine operators. These are supported by the district's Head of Accounting, Robert Baker, responsible for basic operation and business applications, who reports to Ralph Raitt, Business Manager. Robert E. Rolens, Director of Research and Curriculum Consultant is responsible for educational applications. He works with Assistant Superintendent Frank M. Gulick, Head of the Division of Educational Services. All the above report to L. L. Jones, District Superintendent of Schools.

27

WESTCHESTER COUNTY BOARD OF COOPERATIVE EDUCATIONAL
SERVICES (SECOND SUPERVISORY DISTRICT)
Port Chester, New York

40,000 pupils, K–12, in 26 districts
Punched card operations begun in 1962; computer acquired in 1964
Approximate budgeted expenditures for fiscal 1965: not available
Computers owned: none

Westchester BOCES-2 recently installed a computer (U-1004) supported by a small (2-keypunch) installation. Service is provided to participating districts in a number of areas such as fiscal accounting, census, scheduling, attendance, report cards and test scoring. Begun in 1964–65, a two-year senior high curriculum in data processing is presently offered, with courses involving laboratory use of equipment.

BOCES was organized to help cooperating school districts obtain services not readily or economically available to small districts. Data processing is a relatively new service; previous services included a shared teacher program in such areas as art and music and a centralized vocational and special education program.

In data processing, the staff of 6 persons is led by Robert Brophy, Manager, who reports to Bernard L. Bryan, District Superintendent.

Appendix C

Selected Bibliography

AEDS Bulletin, Association for Educational Data Systems, published monthly.

American Association of Collegiate Registrars and Admissions Officers, Joint Committee on Data and Definitions in Higher Education, *Handbook of Data and Definitions in Higher Education,* Washington, D.C.: American Council on Education, 1962.

Atkinson, Richard C., and Hansen, Duncan N., *Computer-assisted Instruction in Initial Reading,* Stanford, Calif.: Institute for Mathematical Studies in the Social Sciences, Stanford University Press, 1966.

"Automated Pupil Attendance Procedures," *Baltimore Bulletin of Education,* Vol. 60, No. 2 (1963).

"Automation at the Central Office," *Educational Executives Overview,* Vol. 3, No. 1 (January 1962).

Beaton, A. E., Jr., "University Data Processing Centers," *Harvard Educational Review,* Vol. 31, No. 3 (1961).

Beattie, A. W., "Thoughts on the Computer and Education," *Data Processing for Education,* Vol. 1, No. 2 (December 1962).

Bendick, Marc, "Equipment for Automated Teaching," *Datamation,* Vol. 7, No. 4 (April 1961).

Bergstein, Harold, "The Computer-based Classroom," *Datamation,* Vol. 7, No. 4 (April 1961).

Berkeley, E. C., and Lovett, L. L., *Glossary of Terms in Computers and Data Processing,* Newtonville, Mass.: Berkeley Enterprises, 1960.

Berry, W. M., "An Electronic Payroll," *Educational Executives Overview* (May 1960).

"Better Processing of Educational Data," *American School Board Journal,* Vol. 143, No. 3 (September 1961).

Bitzer, Donald L., and Braunfeld, P. G., "Computer Teaching Machines Projects PLATO and ILLIAC," *Computers and Automation*, Vol. 11, No. 2 (February 1962).

Bitzer, Donald L., and Braunfeld, P. G., "PLATO: An Automatic Teaching Device," *IRE Transactions on Education* (December 1961).

Borko, Howard, *et al, Computer Applications in the Behavioral Sciences*, Englewood Cliffs, N.J.: Prentice-Hall, 1962.

Bush, R. N., "Using Machines to Make the High School Schedule," *School Review*, Vol. 69, No. 1 (Spring 1961).

Bushnell, Don D., *The Automation of School Information Systems*, DAVI Monograph No. 1 (1964).

——, "Computers in Education," *Computers and Automation*, Vol. 12, No. 3 (March 1963).

——, "The Role of the Computer in Future Instructional Systems," *AV Communication Review*, Vol. 11, No. 2 (1963).

Business Week (February 1, 1964).

Caleo, R. L., "What You Can Learn from the World's Biggest User of EDP," *Administrative Management*, Vol. 23, No. 10 (October 1962).

Careers in Electronic Data Processing, Project on Information Processing, Washington, D.C.: National Science Teachers Association, 1962.

Cerne, Al, and Logan, Jack, *Olathe Public Schools Presents Data Processing*, Olathe, Kansas: Olathe Public Schools, 1962.

Cogswell, John F., and Bushnell, Don D., "A Computer-based Laboratory for Automation in School Systems," *Audio Visual Communication Review* (July–August, 1961).

Colmey, J. W., "Automation, How Much and How Soon for Your District?" *The Nation's Schools*, Vol. 70, No. 4 (October 1962).

"Computer-based Laboratory for Learning and Teaching," *Automated Education Letter*, Vol. 1, No. 1 (October 1965).

Computer Oriented Mathematics, Washington, D.C.: National Council of Teachers of Mathematics, 1963.

"Computers and Educational Research," *Harvard Education Review*, Vol. 31, No. 3 (Summer 1961).

Computers in Instruction, Washington, D.C.: National Education Association (no date).

Conway, B., Gibbons, J., and Watts, D. E., *Business Experience with Electronic Computers*, New York: Controllers Institute Research Foundation, 1959.

Coulson, J. E., *Programmed Learning and Computer Based Instruction*, New York: John Wiley & Sons, 1962.

Counce, S., and Davis, R. E., "Data Processing in a Large School System," *Bulletin of the National Association of Secondary-School Principals*, Vol. 47, No. 280 (February 1963).

Coyle, F., "Data Processing in Schools, Where?" *Data Processing for Education*, Vol. 1, No. 1 (November 1962).

Crisler, R. D., and Wogaman, T. D., "Educational Data Processing at Richmond," *Journal of Secondary Education*, Vol. 38, No. 2 (February 1963).

"Data Processing and Computer Courses at Colleges and Universities," Data Processing Yearbook 1962–1963, Detroit: American Data Processing, 1962.

Data Processing Information, New York: International Business Machines (March 1964).

"Data Processing at the Memphis Schools with the IBM 1401 and Ramac 305," *General Information Manual*, New York: International Business Machines, 1963.

Data Processing Procedures, Langhorne, Pa.: Neshaminy School District, 1962.

Data Processing Progress Report, 1962–1963, Liverpool, N.Y.: Liverpool Central School District, 1963.

Dombrow, R. T., "A Study of Manual and Machine Techniques for Processing Clerical Data in a Secondary School of 1,000 Students," unpublished doctoral dissertation, Philadelphia, Pa.: Temple University, 1960.

Edgerton, Germeshausen, and Grier, Inc., *Survey of College Data Processing Machines, Courses, and Degrees*, Report No. L–634, AEC No. 1183–1008 (December 20, 1963).

Educational Data Processing: Introduction to the Punched Card, Concord, N.H.: State Education Department, 1963.

Electronic Data Processing–I, Technical Education Program Series No. 4, Washington, D.C.: U.S. Government Printing Office, 1963.

Electronic Data Processing as Applied to Educational Records, Milwaukee, Wis.: Milwaukee Public Schools, 1962.

Electronic Data Processing Suggested 2-Year Post–High School Curriculum for Computer Programmer and Business Application Analysts, U.S. Department of Health, Education, and Welfare, OE–80024, Washington, D.C.: U.S. Government Printing Office, 1963.

"Employment Outlook for Electronic Computer Operating Personnel and for Programmers," *BLS Bulletin,* Bulletin No. 1300–34, Publication 8361, Washington, D.C.: U.S. Government Printing Office, April 1962.

Englund, D., and Estavan, D., "Programming a Computer to Teach," *Datamation,* Vol. 7, No. 4 (April 1961).

Evans, L. H., "Educational Implications of Automation," *Newsletter,* American Documentation Institute, Vol. 1, No. 4–NS (June 1962).

————, "The Schools and Automation," *CTA Journal,* Vol. 58, No. 6 (October 1962).

————, and Arnstein, G. E., eds., *Automation and the Challenge to Education,* Publication 721–18804, Washington, D.C.: National Education Association (September 1962).

Fein, Louis, "The Role of the University in Computers, Data Processing, and Related Fields," *Communications of the Association for Computer Machinery,* Vol. 2, No. 9 (September 1959).

Finn, J. D., and Perrin, D. C., *Bibliography on New Media and Instructional Technology,* Washington, D.C.: National Education Association, 1962.

Flanagan, S., "Machine Programming at Huntington Beach High School," *Journal of Secondary Education,* Vol. 36, No. 6 (October 1961).

Fleming, A. S., "Automation and Education," *NEA Journal,* Vol. 51, No. 7 (October 1962).

Flowers, A. W., "Optical Scanner Approach to Attendance Accounting on the Secondary Level," *Data Processing for Education,* Vol. 1, No. 2 (December 1962).

————, "What School Administrators Need to Know About Electronic Data Processing," *Data Processing for Education,* Vol. 1, No. 1 (November 1962).

————, and Kinsman, I. J., *Electronic Data Processing in the Modern High School,* Phoenix, Ariz.: Phoenix Public Schools, 1962.

Foster, C. C., "Using a Computer for Non-conflict Scheduling of High School Classes," *Michigan Education Journal,* Vol. 40, No. 8 (December 1962).

Freeman, J. P., "Starting an Electronic Data Processing Program in a School System," *American School Board Journal,* Vol. 146, No. 2 (February 1963).

Gallagher, J. D., *Management Information Systems and the Computer,* New York: American Management Association, 1961.

Gerletti, R. C., "Electronic Data Processing Applied to AV Centers," *Audiovisual Instruction,* Vol. 6, No. 10 (December 1961).

Goldwyn, A. J., "Information Retrieval: The Man-Machine Interface," *Data Processing for Education,* Vol. 2, No. 11 (1963).

Gotlieb, Calvin C., and Hume, J. N. P., *High Speed Data Processing,* New York: McGraw-Hill, 1958.

Gregory, R. H., and Van Horn, R. L., *Automatic Data Processing Systems: Principles and Procedures,* San Francisco: Wadsworth, 1960.

Grossman, Alvin, "Data Processing—An Answer to the Shackles of Paper Work and Decision Making," *Bulletin of the National Association of Secondary-School Principals,* Vol. 46, No. 273 (April 1962).

————, ed., *Journal of Educational Data Processing,* Sacramento, Calif.: Research and Development Center in Educational Data Processing, Educational Systems Corporation.

————, "New Approach to Guidance Research Using an Electronic Computer," *California Journal of Education Research,* Vol. 13, No. 4 (September 1962).

————, "A Report of a Study—Processing Pupil Personnel Data," *California State Department of Education Bulletin,* Vol. 31, No. 2 (March 1962).

Gruenberger, Fred, "Computer Training and Education," *Datamation,* Vol. 9, No. 5 (May 1963).

————, "The Role of Secondary Schools in Computer Education," *Report of the Conference on Computer Oriented Mathematics and the Secondary School,* Washington, D.C.: National Council of Teachers of Mathematics (May 1963).

Gruman, Allen J., *High School Records and Services Facilitated by the Use of Punched Cards,* unpublished doctoral dissertation, Los Angeles: University of Southern California, 1958.

Haga, E. J., "EDP and the Educator: Sources," *Business Education World,* Vol. 39, No. 9 (May 1959).

Hall, J., *Computers in Education,* New York: Pergamon Press, 1962.

Hamblen, John W., ed., *Educational Data Processing Newsletter,* Carbondale, Ill.: Educational Data Systems Corporation, Data Processing and Computing Center, Southern Illinois University.

143

Hilton, M. E., ed., *Guidance in the Age of Automation,* Syracuse, N.Y.: Syracuse University Press, 1957.

"How to Teach Data Processing in Your School," *School Management,* Vol. 7, No. 4 (May 1963).

Joplin, H. B., "Plan Better for Electronic Data Processing," *NAA Bulletin,* Vol. 44, No. 5 (January 1963).

Kornfield, L., "What Every School Man Should Know About Data Processing," *School Management,* Vol. 6, Nos. 10–11 (October–November 1962).

"Machine Accounting and Related Services for School Administrators," *The Nation's Schools,* Vol 61, No. 5 (May 1958).

McNerney, J. P., *Installing and Using an Automatic Data Processing System,* Cambridge, Mass.: Harvard University Press, 1961.

Matthies, L. H., *Systemate Before You Automate,* Systemation Seminar, Tulsa, Okla.: Ross-Martin Co.

Mauch, James, "A Systems Analysis Approach to Education," *Phi Delta Kappan,* Vol. 43, No. 4 (January 1962).

Miles, E. P., and Hartford, D. L., *A Study of Administrative Uses of Computers in Colleges and Universities,* Tallahassee, Fla.: Florida State University Press, 1962.

Mitzel, Harold E., and Wodtke, Kenneth H., "The Development and Presentation of Four Different College Courses by Computer Teleprocessing," *Interim Report,* U.S. Office of Education–sponsored project, Title VII, Part B, NDEA Act of 1958, University Park, Pa.: Computer–assisted Instruction Laboratory, College of Education, Pennsylvania State University (June 1965).

Modern Data Processing Methods for Pupil Accounting in Maine, Augusta, Me.: State Department of Education, 1962.

Murphy, Judith, and Sutter, Robert, *School Scheduling by Computer,* New York: Educational Facilities Laboratories, 1964.

Murphy, R. M., "Data Processing System for the Small High School," *Bulletin of the National Association of Secondary-School Principals,* Vol. 46, No. 273 (April 1962).

National Conference of Professors of Educational Administration, *Automation, Its Meaning for Educational Administration,* New York: Bureau of Publications, Teachers College, Columbia University, 1957.

Nett, Roger, and Hetzler, S. A., *An Introduction to Electronic Data Processing,* Glencoe, Ill.: Free Press of Glencoe, 1959.

Oakford, R. V. "Machine Assistance for Constructing the High School

Schedule: An Industrial Engineer's Report," *Journal of Secondary Education*, Vol. 36, No. 6 (October 1961).

O'Toole, John F., Jr., "Systems Analysis: A Rational Approach to Decision-making in Education," *SDC Magazine*, Vol. 8, No. 7 (July 1965).

Patton, Stanley R., *Progress Report on Total Information Service*, Chicago: Bureau of Data Processing, Chicago Public Schools, May 1963.

Postley, J. A., *Computers and People*, New York: McGraw-Hill, 1960.

"Processing Educational Data on Punched Card Equipment," *California Schools*, Vol. 31, No. 10 (October 1960).

Project on Information Processing Newsletter, Vol. 1, No. 5 (November 1963).

"Public Education Records," *General Information Manual*, New York: International Business Machines, 1962.

Pullen, Charles K., "State Department of Education—The Key to Educational Data Processing," *Data Processing for Education*, Vol. 2, Nos. 1 and 2 (1963).

Punched Card Equipment in Schools, Miami, Fla.: Dade County Public Schools, 1962.

Reed, Luton, R., *Data Processing Systems: A Guide for Educational Administrators*, Central New York School Study Council, 1964.

Report of an Experiment: The State Pilot Project in Educational Data Processing, Richmond, Calif.: Richmond City Schools, July 1964.

"Roster of School, College, and University Computer Centers," *Computers and Automation*, Vol. 11, No. 6 (June 1962).

Rowan, Thomas C., "Cybernation and Society: An Overview," *SDC Magazine*, Vol. 8, No. 9 (September 1965).

Russell, O. C., "Data Processing for Smaller Districts," *School Management*, Vol. 4, No. 4 (April 1960).

Saathoff, A. B., "Automation in School Accounting," *American School Board Journal*, Vol. 142, No. 3 (March 1961).

Schools Conducting Title VIII Preparatory or Extension Data Processing Technology Courses, Technical Education Branch, U.S. Office of Education, Washington, D.C.: U.S. Government Printing Office, December 1962.

Scott, C. R., "Computer as a Tool of Education," *American Business Education*, Vol. 18 (May 1962).

Silberman, H. F., "The Digital Computer in Education," *Phi Delta Kappan*, Vol. 43, No. 8 (May 1962).

Skinner, B. F., "Teaching Machines," *Science,* Vol. 128, No. 3330 (October 1958).

State Plans for Improving Statistical Services, U.S. Department of Health, Education, and Welfare, Bulletin No. 16, OE–20028, Washington, D.C.: U.S. Government Printing Office, 1961.

Stevens, R. D., "Data-Processing: Who Does What?" *Supervisory Management,* Vol. 8, No. 3 (March 1963).

"Storage, Retrieval, and Dissemination of Information," *General Information Manual,* New York: International Business Machines, 1962.

Student Scheduling, Memphis, Tenn.: Department of Instruction, Memphis City Schools, January 1963.

Suppes, Patrick, *Computer-assisted Instruction in the Schools: Potentialities, Problems, Prospects,* Stanford, Calif.: Institute for Mathematical Studies in the Social Sciences, Stanford University Press, 1965.

"Survey of Computer Services," *Computers and Automation,* Vol. 11, No. 6 (June 1962).

Systems and Procedures, A Notebook for the Systems Man, U.S. Treasury Department, Publication No. 460 (2–63), Washington, D.C.: U.S. Government Printing Office, 1963.

Thurston, P. H., "Who Should Control Information Systems?" *Harvard Business Review,* Vol. 40, No. 6 (November–December 1962).

Tussing, R. T., "Consideration of the Place of EDP in the College Curriculum," *Collegiate News and Views* (December 1962).

Use of the IBM 7070 for Student Scheduling, Rochester, N.Y.: Office of Field Service, College of Education, University of Rochester, 1963.

Walker, Virgil R., "The Utilization of Machine Punched Card Procedures in Large Public School Systems," unpublished doctoral dissertation, Minneapolis, Minn.: University of Minnesota, 1957.

Weeks, R. P., ed., *Machines and Man,* New York: Appleton-Century-Crofts, 1961.

Whitlock, James W., *Automatic Data Processing in Education,* New York: Macmillan, 1964.

Index

147

demic degrees, 24–25; criteria for funding projects, 89–92; recommendations for future, 92–101
Richmond (Calif.) EDP Center, 53
Richmond (Calif.) Union High School: 77; SOCRATES, 77
Rochester (N.Y.) Public Schools, 134

St. Louis junior college district, 80
San Jose (Calif.) high school, 78
Scheduling: 58, 72, 76–78, 95–96; in colleges, 76; in secondary schools, 77–78, 95
Scheduling of Classes Realized Automatically Through Effortless Systemization (SOCRATES), 77
School administration: 21–24, 53–54, 59–64, 71–74; business management, 33; general, 63; general business accounting. See Business accounting; instructional programs, 63–64; simulation techniques, 80; student accounting, 61–62, 72
School Mathematics Study Group (SMSG), 13
School organization, 16–18, 96
Schools Conducting Title VIII Preparatory or Extension Data Processing Technology Courses, 82
Schwab, Joseph, 13
Sciences: 6, 33, 36; in curricula, 14
Secondary schools: 4, 11, 62, 73, 78, 81, 95; computer education, 81, 82, 83, 84; mathematics, 33; scheduling, 77–78, 95; simulation techniques, 80; student accounting, 61
Service bureau facilities, 40, 50
Shaker Heights (Ohio) Public Schools, 134–35
Simulation techniques: 7, 17; in business, 7–8; in education, 17, 75, 77, 80, 97; in industry, 7–8
Skinner, B. F., 14
Software: 5, 42–46, 93; for computer installations, 38, 42, 45–46, 93; costs, 5, 46, 93; for punched

card installations, 43–45. See also Punched card processing
Sorter, 36, 41, 42
Stanford Institute for Mathematical Studies in the Social Sciences, 65
Stanford University School of Education, 65, 77, 81, 97
State education agencies, 35, 58, 70
Statistics, teaching of, 67, 68
Storing devices, computer, 38
Student accounting, 61–62, 72
Student attendance, 39, 53, 71
Student personnel records, 57, 59, 71, 74, 94
Student progress records, 66, 72–73, 79, 80
Student Records, procedure, 67
Suppes, Patrick, 65
System Development Corporation (SDC), CLASS, 67–68, 77(n), 78–79, 80

Tabulator, 37, 49
Teaching machine, 64
Team teaching, 16–17, 19, 31, 78, 97
Teleprocessing, 52, 67, 68
Teletypewriter, 68
Test scoring machine, 35, 39, 42, 58
TINT, 68
Title V, Elementary and Secondary Education Act, 35, 84
Title VIII, National Defense Education Act, 82, 84
Title X, National Defense Education Act, 34
Total Information Service (TIS), 70–72
Tulsa County (Okla.) Independent School District No. 1, 135

Unit record, 35, 36, 82
U.S. Office of Education: 34–35, 80, 100–01; BEDS, 54; Cooperative Research Program, 34, 68, 87; Elementary and Secondary Education Act, 35, 84; National Defense Education Act, 34, 35, 82, 84

A 6
B 7
C 8
D 9
E 0
F 1
G 2
H 3
I 4
J 5